Orange Line
2

von
Jennifer Baer-Engel
Manfred Bojes
Marion Horner
Bernadette Kesting
Mary Jo Rabe
Geoffrey Sammon

Herausgeber: Frank Haß

Ernst Klett Schulbuchverlage
Stuttgart Leipzig

Steckbrief

My name: _____

My address: _____

_____

My phone number: _____

My school: _____

My class: _____

Die folgenden Arbeitsanweisungen findest du in diesem *Workbook*. Falls du dir mal nicht ganz sicher bist, was du bei einer Übung tun sollst, kannst du in dieser Liste nachschauen.

Ganz hinten im Heft findest du die Lösungen zu den Aufgaben der *Check-out*-Seiten. Damit kannst du selber deine Arbeit überprüfen. Aber erst die Übungen bearbeiten, dann nachschauen!

Check … .	Überprüfe … .
Choose the correct information.	Wähle die richtige Information.
Compare … .	Vergleiche … .
Complete the grid/the rhymes/the mindmap.	Vervollständige die Tabelle/die Reime/die Mindmap.
Correct the sentences.	Korrigiere die Sätze.
Describe … .	Beschreibe … .
Fill in the missing words.	Füge die fehlenden Wörter ein.
Find the correct pairs.	Finde die richtigen Paare.
Finish the definitions.	Schreibe die Definitionen zu Ende.
Give the opposites.	Gib das Gegenteil an.
Guess the correct word.	Errate das richtige Wort.
Help each other.	Helft einander.
Listen to the text.	Hör dir den Text an.
Look at the list.	Schau dir die Liste an.
Look for … .	Suche … .
Look up the words in the dictionary.	Schlage die Wörter im Wörterbuch nach.
Make a ✓ for ‚yes' and a ✗ for ‚no'.	Mach ein ✓ für ‚ja' und ein ✗ für ‚nein'.
Make notes about … .	Mach Notizen zu … .
Make notes/sentences.	Mach Notizen/Sätze.
Make up a story.	Erfinde eine Geschichte.
Point to … .	Zeige auf … .
Put … together.	Füge … zusammen.
Put a ✓ in the correct box.	Mach ein ✓ in das richtige Kästchen.
Put the correct words in the puzzle.	Setze die richtigen Wörter in das Rätsel ein.
Put the words/the sentences in the right order.	Bringe die Wörter/Sätze in die richtige Reihenfolge.
Underline the key words.	Unterstreiche die Schlüsselwörter.
Work with a partner.	Arbeite mit einem Partner zusammen.
Write a ✓ for ‚yes' and a ✗ for ‚no'.	Schreibe ein ✓ für ‚ja' und ein ✗ für ‚nein'.
Write down the right meaning.	Schreibe die richtige Bedeutung auf.

| | Sprachenpass | **S** |

Mein Sprachenpass

> Hallo!
> Hattest du auch so tolle Ferien wie ich? Was hast du alles unternommen? Ich war den Sommer über in Irland, da musste ich natürlich die ganze Zeit Englisch sprechen. Über Irland erfährst du später noch mehr. Vielleicht hast du das, was du auf Englisch schon kannst, auch in den Ferien verwenden können? Nimm dir doch ein bisschen Zeit und fülle wieder deinen Sprachenpass aus!

Wo hast du in den Ferien etwas auf Englisch gehört oder gelesen?
_____

Hast du auch Englisch gesprochen? Wenn ja, welche Wörter hast du besonders oft benutzt?
_____

Welche DVDs hast du schon auf Englisch gesehen?
_____

Welches englische Lied gefällt dir besonders gut?
_____

Welche englischen Internet-Seiten hast du dir angeschaut?
_____

> Jetzt kannst du wieder aufschreiben, welche Ziele du dir für das kommende Schuljahr im Fach Englisch vornehmen willst.

Ich möchte folgendes noch besser können:
_____

Dafür werde ich folgendes tun:
_____

Datum: _____ Unterschrift: _____

three **3**

Unit 1   Back to school

1 About school (→ p. 11/ex. 1)

Write the sentences under the correct photos.

Registration is with the class teacher.
There are lockers for the pupils' bags.

Pupils must be in the assembly hall before 8:35.
The school shop opens before school.

1. *There are lockers for the pupils' bags.*

2. *The school shop opens before school.*

3. *Registration is with the class teacher.*

4. *Pupils must be in the assembly hall before 8:35.*

2 The names of lessons (→ p. 11/ex. 1)

Make the names of lessons with the letters.

1. sMtah
2. trA
3. cTnyoloegh
4. ioHsrty
5. erapgohGy
6. eiSncec

1. *Maths*
2. *Art*
3. *Technology*
4. *History*
5. *Geography*
6. *Science*

3 Let's listen: Love or hate? (→ p. 11/ex. 3)

Put ✔ in the correct box.

1. Science is on   ☐ Friday morning.   ✔ Friday afternoon.
2. Miss Brown doesn't like ✔ mice.   ☐ Pete.
3. Mr Marco gives   ✔ a lot of homework.   ☐ boring lessons.
4. Kate loves   ✔ Italian.   ☐ German.
5. Sue thinks Laura is   ☐ cool.   ✔ stupid.

4 four

| | Check-in | Language | Story | Wordwise | Check-out | | 1 |

4 SKILLS: Notes (→ p. 11/ex. 2)

a) Read what Terry says.
Underline the key words¹ and phrases.

The school day starts with <u>registration</u> or <u>assembly</u> at <u>8:35</u>. Registration is in the <u>classroom</u> with our <u>class teacher</u>, and assembly is in the <u>assembly hall</u> with <u>all the Year Eight pupils</u>.

Then we go to our <u>lessons</u>. We have lessons in the <u>morning</u> and in the <u>afternoon</u>, and we often use <u>computers</u>. For lunch we can bring <u>sandwiches</u> or buy <u>food</u> in the <u>cafeteria</u>.

Of course we must always wear the correct <u>uniform</u> – a <u>Tallis T-shirt or sweatshirt</u> with <u>black trousers or a skirt</u>. We buy our <u>uniform</u> in the <u>school shop</u>. The <u>shop</u> opens <u>before school</u> and <u>at lunchtime</u>. It sells <u>pens</u> and <u>pencils</u>, too, and also the <u>Tallis PE kit</u>. We've all got <u>lockers</u> where we put our <u>PE kit</u> and our <u>school bags</u>.

b) Use your key words from a) and make notes about Thomas Tallis.
Write your notes in the correct place in the grid on this page.

c) Complete the grid with notes about your school. *(Lösungsvorschlag)*

	Thomas Tallis	My school
registration	8:35 – in classroom – class teacher	8:00 – in classroom
assembly	8:35 – in assembly hall – all the Year Eight pupils	no assembly
lessons	in the morning – in the afternoon – use computers	in the morning – in the afternoon
lunch	bring sandwiches – buy food – in cafeteria	bring sandwiches
uniform	Tallis T-shirt or sweatshirt – black trousers or skirt	no uniform
school shop	before school – at lunchtime – pens – pencils – Tallis PE kit	no school shop
lockers	PE kit – school bags	no lockers

d) Compare Thomas Tallis with your school.

1. What is the same? Write two sentences.

   We also have registration at our school. We have lessons in the morning and in the afternoon.

   _____

2. What is different? Write two sentences.

   We don't have lockers at our school. There is no school shop or uniform.

   _____

e) What do you think? What is good or not so good at Thomas Tallis? Write down your ideas in your exercise book. *(individuelle Schülerlösung)*

¹key words ['kiː ˌwɜːdz] – *wichtige Wörter*

1 Language

5 A puzzle (→ p. 12/ex. 1)

Put the correct words in the puzzle.

1. At ... the teacher calls the names of all the pupils in the class.
2. PE means ... Education.
3. At Thomas Tallis ... is one of the foreign languages.
4. ... is every day from 10:50 to 11:10.
5. It is Day 8, so the teachers have a ...
6. All the pupils wear a Tallis T-shirt or ...
7. The girls and boys must be in the ... hall before 8:35.
8. RE means ... Education.
9. You must put your bag in your ...
10. Your ... shows when the lessons are.

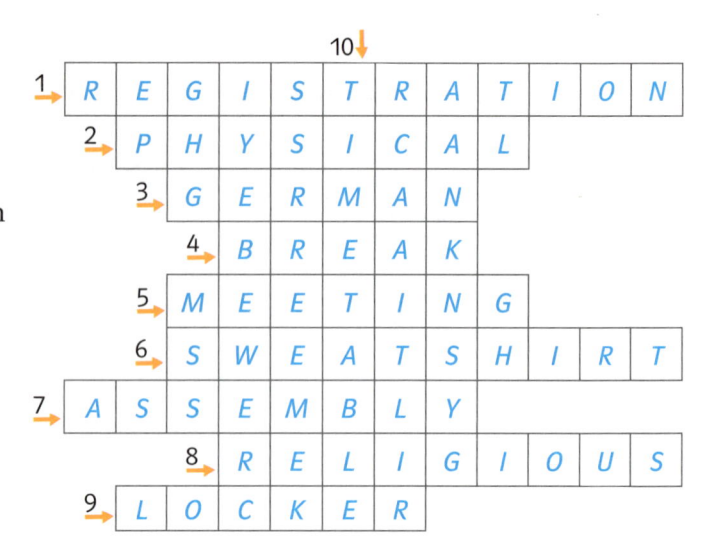

1. REGISTRATION
2. PHYSICAL
3. GERMAN
4. BREAK
5. MEETING
6. SWEATSHIRT
7. ASSEMBLY
8. RELIGIOUS
9. LOCKER

6 Rhymes for the times (→ p. 12/ex. 1)

Complete the rhymes with the words for the times.

1. Look at the time – it's `8:30` _half past eight_ . Come on, hurry up. We don't want to be late!

2. Lesson one always starts at `8:50` _ten to nine_ . I don't like German, but Science is fine.

3. At `13:00` _one o'clock_ _____ on Days Two and Three

   I'm in my favourite lesson, PE.

4. Let's meet in the cafeteria at `13:40` _twenty to two_ _____.

   It's always fun to have lunch with you.

5. It's `15:05` _five past three_ _____ in the afternoon. Great!

   That means we can go home soon.

7 My favourite day at school (→ p. 13/ex. 2)

Put in the correct words.

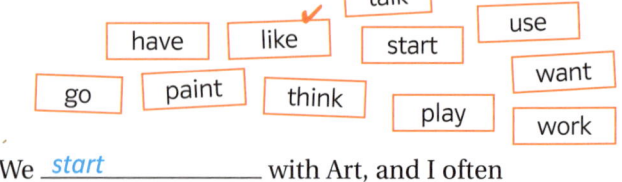

I _like_ all my lessons on Day Ten. We _start_ with Art, and I often

paint funny pictures of my dog. We always _have_ fun in Maths on Day

Ten, too, because we _play_ games with numbers. After break all the pupils in my

class _go_ to the sports hall for a PE lesson. Then in Drama we _talk_

about problems and _do_ role plays. In our last lesson, Geography, we usually

use computers. My friends in other classes often _work_ with

computers in their last lesson of the week, too. I _think_ the teachers _want_

a quiet time on Friday afternoon!

6 six

| Check-in | **Language** | Story | Wordwise | Check-out | | 1 |

8 What do the pupils say about their teachers? (→ p. 13/ex. 2)

Find the correct pairs of ideas and make sentences.

Remember:
*He, she, it –
…**s**/…**es** muss mit!*

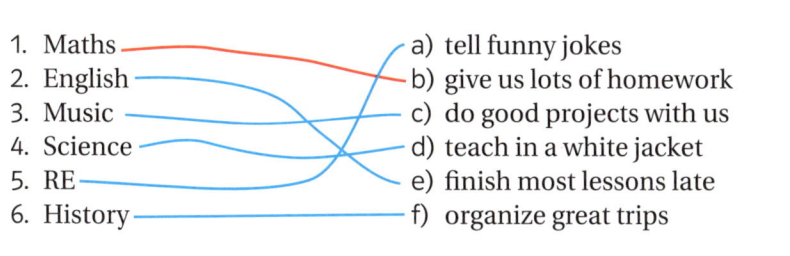

1. Maths — a) tell funny jokes
2. English — b) give us lots of homework
3. Music — c) do good projects with us
4. Science — d) teach in a white jacket
5. RE — e) finish most lessons late
6. History — f) organize great trips

1. Our Maths teacher gives us lots of homework.
2. Our English teacher finishes most lessons late.
3. Our Music teacher does good projects with us.
4. Our Science teacher teaches in a white jacket.
5. Our RE teacher tells funny jokes.
6. Our History teacher organises great trips.

9 In the lunch break (→ p. 13/ex. 2)

Put in the right forms.

Terry: Come on, Emma.

We *(want)* __want__ to play football.

Lisa: Oh, you needn't ask Emma.

She always *(say)* __says__ no.

Emma: Well, when I *(kick)* __kick__ the ball,

it *(go)* __goes__ the wrong way.

Sam: Oh, don't worry. That *(happen)* __happens__ with me, too.

Emma: Yes, but all the time. And Lisa always *(shout)* __shouts__ at me.

Lisa: That's because I *(hate)* __hate__ it when girls *(play)* __play__ like

idiots. It *(look)* __looks__ bad. Other people *(think)* __think__

girls can't play football.

Sam: But Emma *(hate)* __hates__ it when you *(shout)* __shout__ at her.

Lisa: OK, I *(know)* __know__ that now. Sorry, Emma. Play with us. Please.

Terry: Wait, look at the time! German *(start)* __starts__ in a minute. It's too late for

football now.

seven 7

1 | Language

10 What is wrong? (→ p. 14/ex. 1)

Find the wrong words or phrases. Underline them and write the correct words after the sentences.

1. Sam must look for Jake, the new boy. – **look after**
2. Jake has got a great suntan because he is from Italy. – **Australia**
3. Emma is in a hurry, so she wants to have lunch now. – **hungry**
4. They can choose their food from different tables in the cafeteria. – **menus**
5. Terry and Jake are having pizza for lunch. – **fish and chips**

11 Jake's questions (→ p. 14/ex. 2)

Finish what Jake says to his new friends.

- not use many different words
- not know where it is ✓
- not give us too much homework
- not rain every day
- not like his PE shirt
- not close now

1. Can you take me to the school shop, please? I **don't know where it is.**
2. I've got too much in my locker. Look, the door **doesn't close now.**
3. Are the teachers here OK? I hope they **don't give us too much homework.**
4. English in Australia is the same really. We **don't use many different words.**
5. The weather in England isn't so terrible. At least it **doesn't rain every day.**
6. Ha ha, look at Terry's face! I can see he **doesn't like his PE shirt.**

12 Are you good at school, Jake? (→ p. 14/ex. 2)

Put in the correct forms of 'to be'.

| 'm (2x) | am | 'm not | 's | is (2x) | isn't (2x) | are (2x) | aren't (2x) |

Jake: **Is** our timetable the same every week?

Emma: No, it **isn't**. We have a ten-day timetable, and the two weeks **are** different.

Terry: **Are** you good at school, Jake?

Jake: Yes, I **am**. I **'m** always the best pupil in the class!

Emma: Wow! **Is** that true?

Jake: No, of course not! I **'m** good at PE, but I **'m not** so good at other subjects.

Terry: We already know you **aren't** good at English – you use strange words like 'tucker'!

Emma: Hey, Terry! It **isn't** nice to say things like that.

Terry: It **'s** only a joke, silly. But some of Jake's words **aren't** English English!

13 About Australia (→ p. 15/ex. 3)

What do Jake's friends ask about Australia?

| cars | drive |  | your old school | teach |  | Australia | get |  | kids | play |

1. Do cars drive on the left?
2. Does your old school teach German?
3. Does Australia get a lot of rain?
4. Do the kids play basketball?
5. Do people eat fish and chips?
6. Does summer start in December?

| people | eat |
| summer | start |

14 Which? – What? (→ p. 15/ex. 6)

Put in the correct question word. Then answer the question.

1. Which language does Mr Marco teach: Italian or German? – Italian
2. What hobbies does Jake do? – music and surfing
3. What time do lessons start after lunch? – 14:10
4. Which girl is good at football: Emma or Lisa? – Lisa
5. Which subject does Sam hate: Music or Art? – Music
6. On what day can the pupils go home early? – Wednesday

15 Let's listen: A lunch problem (→ p. 15/ex. 6) (HV-Text S. 86)

Listen. Then answer the questions with short answers.

| Yes, she does. | No, he hasn't. | No, he can't. |
| Yes, they have. | Yes, they are. | No, they don't. |

1. Has Sam got the money for his lunch? – No, he hasn't.
2. Can he borrow money from Emma? – No, he can't.
3. Are the pizzas too small for two people? – Yes, they are.
4. Do Emma and Sam choose spaghetti? – No, they don't.
5. Does Mrs Green like Sam? – Yes, she does.
6. Have Sam and Emma got lots of food? – Yes, they have.

nine 9

16 Let's talk: At Thomas Tallis (→ p. 15/ex. 6)

Arbeite mit deinem Partner zusammen. Entscheidet, wer mit Teil A und wer mit Teil B anfängt. Decke den Teil zu, mit dem du nicht arbeitest. Nach einem Durchgang könnt ihr die Rollen tauschen und mit dem anderen Teil arbeiten.

A

Du stellst die Fragen und kontrollierst die Antworten deines Partners mit Hilfe der Lösungen in Klammern.

Where • Jake • live now?

(He lives in England.
He doesn't live in Australia.)

How • Sam and Terry • come to school?

(They come by bike. They don't come by car.)

What • the teachers • say before registration?

(They say 'Good morning'.
They don't say 'G'day'.)

What • Lisa • wear?

(She wears trousers. She doesn't wear a skirt.)

Where • the pupils • have lunch?

(They have lunch in the cafeteria.
They don't have lunch in the classroom.)

What • the school shop • sell?

(It sells pencils.
It doesn't sell chocolate.)

Where • the friends • go on Wednesdays?

(They go to the Drama Club.
They don't go to the Computer Club.)

When • the caretaker • finish his day?

(He finishes at six o'clock.
He doesn't finish at ten past three.)

B

Du kontrollierst die Fragen deines Partners mit Hilfe der Lösungen in Klammern. Die Zeichnungen helfen dir, Antworten zu geben.

(Where does Jake live now?)

(How do Sam and Terry come to school?)

(What do teachers say before registration?)

(What does Lisa wear?)

(Where do the pupils have lunch?)

(What does the school shop sell?)

(Where do the friends go on Wednesdays?)

(When does the caretaker finish his day?)

17 SKILLS: Grammar (→ p. 16/ex. 1)

a) Die folgenden Sätze aus Schülergesprächen enthalten Beispiele im *simple present*.

1. Unterstreiche die Verbformen. Verwende blau für bejahte Aussagen, rot für Verneinung und grün für Fragen.

2. Kreise die Wörter ein, die ausdrücken, wie häufig etwas passiert.

I don't know him.
The new shop sells cool jeans.
He (sometimes) plays Italian music in our lessons.
She doesn't like me.
Does he (often) send you texts?
Do you spend a lot of money (every week)?
I (always) watch the soaps on TV.
We (never) talk.

b) Vervollständige diese *grammar card*.
   1. Setze die richtigen Formeln ein.
   2. Füge konkrete Beispiele aus a) hinzu.

don't + Verb   Verb + s   Does … + Verb
Verb ✓   doesn't + Verb   Do … + Verb

Thema: Wie bilde ich das simple present?

	I, you, we, they	he, she, it
Aussagen	Formel: Verb Beispiel: watch	Formel: Verb + s Beispiel: sells
Verneinung	Formel: don't + Verb Beispiel: don't know	Formel: doesn't + Verb Beispiel: doesn't like
Fragen	Formel: Do + Verb Beispiel: Do you spend	Formel: Does + Verb Beispiel: Does he send

c) Wann verwendest du das *simple present*? Schreibe eine Regel für eine *grammar card*. Lies deine Regel einem Partner vor. Ist die Regel klar? *(individuelle Schülerlösung)*

d) Die Wörter, die du in a) eingekreist hast, sind Signalwörter für das *simple present*. Zeige, wie du sie auf einer *grammar card* sammeln kannst, z. B. mit einem *word star*. *(individuelle Schülerlösung)*

1

✻ 18 School uniform (→ p. 19/ex. 5)

Underline the key words and match the pictures with the texts.

Text	1	2	3	4
Picture	D	B	A	C

1. Wednesday:
 Terry: Hey, look at this <u>poster</u>!
 Emma: Wow! We <u>needn't</u> wear <u>uniform tomorrow</u>.
 Sam: Really? Why? Oh, I see. We bring <u>50p for charity</u>, and then we can wear what we like.
 Emma: I can't wait for tomorrow. I hate school uniform. It's so boring.

2. Thursday morning:
 Emma: Hi! I like your <u>new uniform</u>!
 Terry: Uniform? What do you mean?
 Emma: Well, you're in a <u>red sweatshirt</u>, and –
 Sam: Oh yes, and my <u>sweatshirt is red, too</u>.
 Emma: <u>No sweatshirt</u> for me today! I want to look really cool. So I'm wearing my favourite skirt.

3. Later on Thursday:
 Emma: Is there room for me at your <u>table</u>?
 Sam: Yes, but – oops! Too late!
 Emma: Oh no! There's <u>spaghetti</u> on the <u>chair</u>.
 Terry: Yes, and now it's on your <u>skirt, too</u>!

4. Friday:
 Sam: What are you painting, Emma? A horse?
 Emma: No, silly. Look, it's a <u>tiger</u>!
 Terry: Er – does that mean your <u>skirt</u> is a <u>tiger, too</u>, Emma? Look, you've got a <u>big yellow</u> mark on it.
 Sam: Oh no! A problem with a skirt again!
 Emma: Don't worry. It's only my school skirt, so it's OK.

✻ 19 My Storybook (→ p. 19/ex. 5)

The key words and the pictures can help you to put in the correct information.

On _Wednesday_ Terry, Sam and Emma see a _poster_ at school. Tomorrow they can bring _50 p_ for _charity_. Then they _can_ wear _what they like_. Emma is very happy because she _hates_ school uniform.

The next _day_ Terry and Sam come to school in _red_ sweatshirts. Emma laughs because their _sweatshirts_ are like a new _uniform_. She wants to look _cool_, so she is wearing her favourite _skirt_. At lunchtime she _has spaghetti_ on her beautiful skirt. On Friday Emma is painting a _tiger_, and there is a big yellow _mark_ on her _skirt_ but it is OK.

12 twelve

Check-in   Language   Story   **Wordwise**   Check-out   **1**

20 SKILLS: Definitions (→ p. 20/ex. 1)

Finish the definitions of the red words.

1. Shorts are short _trousers_.
2. Break is the time between _lessons_.
3. When you are sad you are not _happy_.
4. Tomorrow is the day after _today_.
5. When you are hungry you want _food_.
6. In Geography you learn about _countries_.
7. A clue gives you _information_.

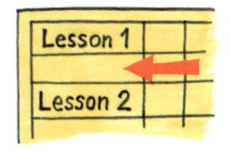

21 Word groups (→ p. 20/ex. 2)

a) One word in every group is wrong. Find it and underline it.
b) Find the word for all the other things in the group. Write the word after the group.

1. train • bus • car • <u>cinema</u> • bike: _transport_
2. Art • <u>assembly</u> • History • RE • Science: _subjects_
3. <u>happy</u> • rainy • hot • sunny • cold: _weather_
4. England • Australia • Greece • Italy • <u>German</u>: _countries_
5. <u>ball</u> • cricket • hockey • surfing • basketball: _sports_
6. fish • fruit • <u>soap</u> • cheese • vegetables: _food_

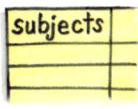

✿ 22 What ideas do the words give you? (→ p. 20/ex. 3)

Write a sentence for every picture.

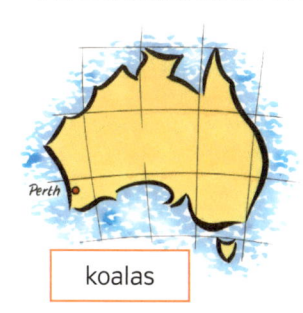

koalas
1. _Koalas live in Australia._

England
3. _It rains a lot in England._

pupils • uniform
2. _Pupils in Germany don't wear uniform._

people • fish and chips
4. _People in England eat fish and chips._

thirteen 13

23 The girls and boys in Jake's class (→ p. 21/ex. 1)

Make sentences with the words and pictures.

1. Tony/hate [maths] lessons
2. Tina and Kate/bring [sandwiches] for lunch
3. Lisa and Emma/love [drama]
4. Terry/go to the  [Rap] Club on Fridays
5. Bob and Steve/play [cards] in the break
6. Sue/come to school on [skates]

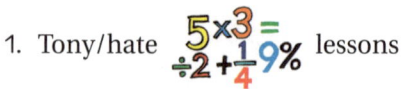

1. _Tony hates Maths lessons._
2. _Tina and Kate bring sandwiches for lunch._
3. _Lisa and Emma love drama._
4. _Terry goes to the Rap Club on Fridays._
5. _Bob and Steve play cards in the break._
6. _Sue comes to school on skates._

24 In Terry's shed (→ p. 21/ex. 2)

Put in: 'do' – 'don't' – 'does' – 'doesn't'.

Jake: Why _do_ you play your drums here in the shed, Terry?

Terry: Because my mother _doesn't_ like the noise in the house.

Jake: _Do_ your parents use the shed, too?

Terry: No, they _don't_. It's my shed. That's why there's a 'Keep out' sign on the door.

Jake: But _doesn't_ your cat come into the shed?

Terry: Yes, she _does_ – but only when I _don't_ play the drums. She's like my mother. She _doesn't_ know good music when she hears it!

25 What does Jake ask his new friends? (→ p. 21/ex. 3)

Which …?
What …?

1. _What_ information can you give me about Greenwich?
2. _What_ sports can you do here?
3. _Which_ way is the Thames from here: north or south?
4. _What_ shops are there in Greenwich?
5. _Which_ word means shirt: Cutty or Sark?

Unit 2   What a week!

1 I'd like to (→ p. 23/ex. 1)

Make three dialogues.   **I'd like to • I'd rather**

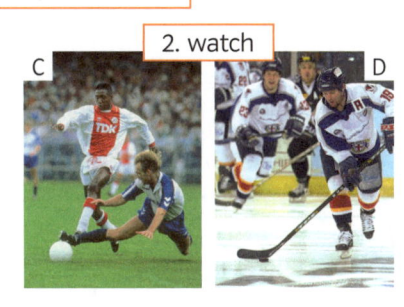

1. go to   2. watch   3. visit

1. A: _I'd like to go to Harrods._

   B: _No! I'd rather go to Camden Market._

2. C: _I'd like to watch football._

   D: _No! I'd rather watch ice hockey._

3. E: _I'd like to visit the Science Museum._

   F: _No! I'd rather visit the zoo._

2 Pictures and numbers (→ p. 23/ex. 1)

Find the correct picture, write down the numbers and say the sentences.

1. The number _37_ bus goes to the ice rink.
2. Tickets for the game are _5_ pounds _50_.
3. A bottle of water? That's _75_ pence, please.
4. I'm looking for seat number _44_.
5. Great! Our number _18_ has got a goal!

3 Let's listen: Plans for the weekend (→ p. 23/ex. 3)

Finish the words in these sentences.

1. Terry's dad has got t_ickets_ for the A_rena_.
2. Emma gets her p_ocket_ money t_omorrow_.
3. Emma must get a b_irthday_ present for her g_randma_.
4. Jade wants to see the baby e_lephant_ at the z_oo_.
5. Sam wants to see the p_lanes_ in the S_cience_ Museum.
6. Terry and Sam can take Sam's m_um_ to the ice rink on S_aturday_.

2 — Language

4 The weekend (→ p. 24/ex. 1)

a) Match the questions and answers.

1. How was Terry's weekend? — It was great.
2. Why were Sam and Terry surprised? — The London Knights were very good.
3. What was the problem for Sam's mum? — Jade was horrible.
4. Where was Emma? — She was at the zoo with Lisa and Jade.
5. When were the girls at the zoo? — They were there on Saturday.
6. Why were Emma and Lisa fed up? — She was cold.

b) Work with a partner. Ask and answer the questions in a).

5 Problems for visitors to London (→ p. 25/ex. 4)

What was the problem for these visitors to London last weekend?

open | good ✓ | free | cheap | very big | quiet

1. "It's raining again!" – The weather _wasn't good._
2. "I'm still hungry. You, too?" – Their sandwiches _weren't very big._
3. "London shows are so expensive!" – Their tickets _weren't cheap._
4. "Oh, we can't see the animals today!" – The zoo _wasn't open._
5. "What a noise! I can't sleep." – His room _wasn't quiet._
6. "It isn't so much fun downstairs on the bus." – The seats upstairs _weren't free._

6 What is your answer? (→ p. 25/ex. 5)

Yes, I was. | No, I wasn't. (Lösungsvorschlag)

1. Were you late for school last week? – _No, I wasn't._
2. Were you with your friends at the weekend? – _Yes, I was._
3. Were you still in bed at six o'clock this morning? – _No, I wasn't._
4. Were you horrible when you were a little child? – _Yes, I was._

7 In the park (→ p. 25/ex. 5)

Put in: was – wasn't – were – weren't

Mrs Taylor: How _was_ it in the park today, Lisa?
Were there a lot of other dogs?

Lisa: No, there _weren't_. There _was_ only one other dog in the park.

Mrs Taylor: Only one? _Was_ it a nice friend for Barker?

Lisa: No, it _wasn't_. It _was_ a horrible animal. And the two boys with it _were_ horrible, too. So it _wasn't_ a good morning for Barker and me.

8 The trip to London Zoo (→ p. 26/ex. 1)

Put in the correct past forms. You can check your answers in Emma's e-mail on page 26 in your book. Look for the sentences with the same information.

| was (2x) | were | bought | left | gave | fell (2x) | went (2x) | threw |
| saw | had | sat | found | ate |

Last Saturday Emma __went__ to London Zoo with Lisa. Lisa's parents __were__ in the café so Lisa __had__ her little sister Jade for the day. They __bought__ the tickets and __went__ in. Lisa __gave__ Jade an apple. But the apple __fell__ on the ground and a pig __ate__ it. Jade __found__ a stick and __threw__ it at the pig. But a zookeeper __saw__ her and he __was__ very angry. Later in the afternoon they __sat__ down on a bridge. Jade's hat __fell__ in the river. It __was__ too difficult to get it, so they __left__ the hat there.

9 Past times (→ p. 26/ex. 1)

Put the 'time' words and phrases in the right order. Go back from the present to the past.

last week, yesterday, three months ago, today ✓, last year, two days ago

- today
- yesterday
- two days ago
- last week
- three months ago
- last year

10 A birthday present for Mr Jackson (→ p. 26/ex. 2)

a) *Read the text. There are twelve past forms. Find them and underline them in red.*

b) *Which verbs do they come from? Put in the correct forms.*

The day before Mr Jackson's birthday last month Terry <u>took</u> his money from his piggy bank and <u>went</u> to Camden Market. There <u>were</u> a lot of good stalls. First Terry <u>saw</u> a cool torch. But his father already <u>had</u> a torch. After that he <u>found</u> a really funny T-shirt. But when Terry <u>read</u> the price he <u>left</u> the T-shirt there. Too expensive! Half an hour later Terry <u>came</u> to the stall where he <u>bought</u> his dad's present. The next day he <u>gave</u> the present to Mr Jackson. What <u>was</u> it? A cricket cap – a great idea for the number one cricket fan in England!

1. take
2. go
3. be
4. see
5. have
6. find
7. read
8. leave
9. come
10. buy
11. give
12. be

11 SKILLS: Collecting irregular past forms (→ p. 26/ex. 2)

a) Vergleiche die Grundform und die *simple past*-Form der Verben. Unterstreiche die Buchstaben, die bei der *simple past*-Form anders sind und die du dir besonders merken musst.
Beispiel: buy – b<u>ought</u>

1. g<u>i</u>ve – g<u>a</u>ve
2. c<u>o</u>me – c<u>a</u>me
3. f<u>a</u>ll – f<u>e</u>ll
4. thr<u>ow</u> – thr<u>ew</u>
5. <u>eat</u> – <u>ate</u>
6. l<u>eave</u> – l<u>eft</u>

> Sometimes only one letter ist different.
> Sometimes a lot of letters are different.

b) Trage die Formen von a) in die *grammar card* ein und schreibe deine eigenen Beispielsätze dazu. Verwende eine andere Farbe für die *simple past*-Formen, damit sie jedesmal auffallen, wenn du deine *grammar card* liest.

Irregular simple past forms *(Lösungsvorschlag)*

verb	simple past	example sentence
buy	bought	Yesterday she bought a pen.
give	gave	Yesterday Lisa gave Jade an apple.
come	came	Yesterday she came home late.
fall	fell	Yesterday the hat fell in the river.
throw	threw	Yesterday she threw a stick.
eat	ate	Yesterday the pig ate an apple.
leave	left	Yesterday they left the hat there.

12 SKILLS: Learning with rhymes (→ p. 26/ex. 2)

a) Vervollständige diese Reime mit den richtigen *simple past*-Formen.

b) Versuche, die Reime auswendig zu lernen.
Kannst du den Reim sagen, wenn dein Partner dir nur das erste Wort (*go, write* usw.) sagt?

sat • went ✓ • read • wrote • saw • took

1. *Go* into the 
   The past is: went.

2. *Write* a 
   The past is: wrote.

3. *Take* your 
   The past is: took.

4. *Sit* on your 
   The past is: sat.

5. *Read* comics in 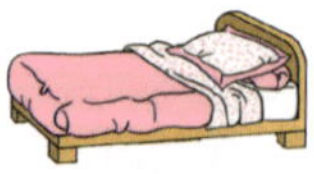
   The past is: read.

6. *See* the sign on the 
   The past is: saw.

| Check-in | **Language** | Story | Wordwise | Check-out | **2** |

13 Last Saturday in the park (→ p. 27/ex. 3)

Write the correct sentences under the pictures. Two sentences are wrong!

A dog found an old shoe in the park. • A child's ice-cream fell on the ground. •
A boy gave a girl some flowers from the park. • A dog came to the park on a skateboard. •
Two girls had fun on their bikes. • A girl and a boy wrote their names on a tree. •
A man sat down on a woman's hat. • Some children threw their shoes into the water.

1. A man sat down on a woman's hat.
2. A boy gave a girl some flowers from the park.
3. Some children threw their shoes into the water.
4. A dog came to the park on a skateboard.
5. A child's ice-cream fell on the ground.
6. Two girls had fun on their bikes.

14 Last week was great (→ p. 27/ex. 3)

Write down what Jake tells his friends.

Monday: find some money under my bed
Tuesday: buy a great CD
Wednesday: eat a big pizza
Thursday: read my new music magazine
Friday: see my favourite TV show
Saturday: go to a football match
Sunday: have a party for my friends

1. On Monday I found some money under my bed.
2. On Tuesday I bought a great CD.
3. On Wednesday I ate a big pizza.
4. On Thursday I read my new music magazine.
5. On Friday I saw my favourite TV show.
6. On Saturday I went to a football match.
7. On Sunday I had a party for my friends.

But you know about the party already — because you were there!

nineteen **19**

15 Present or past forms? (→ p. 27/ex. 3)

One form in every group is different from the others. Find it and underline it.

1. saw • were • took • <u>goes</u>
2. am • <u>had</u> • buys • write
3. throw • are • <u>came</u> • finds
4. <u>give</u> • fell • ate • left

16 Yesterday at school (→ p. 27/ex. 4)

Why were these pupils in trouble with their teachers? Write a sentence for every picture.

1. In Science: She wrote a text message.

2. In Maths: He read a magazine.

3. In Technology: They threw pencil cases.

4. In Geography: He laughed and fell off the chair.

5. In English: They ate sandwiches.

6. In Art: She had a mouse in her bag.

17 Let's listen: What Sam tells Lisa (→ p. 27/ex. 4) (HV-Text S. 86)

Choose the correct information from A and B and complete the sentences.

When you listen, ask: Who? What? Where? When?

A	B
Sam and Terry	ate a lot of cheese.
Grandma	came out of a picture.
A man	had fun in the park.
Jake and Sam	came into Sam's room.
Sam	went to the cinema.

1. On Saturday Jake and Sam had fun in the park.

2. Yesterday afternoon Sam and Terry went to the cinema.

3. Yesterday evening Sam ate a lot of cheese.

4. In Sam's dream a man came out of a picture.

5. At seven o'clock this morning Grandma came into Sam's room.

18 Let's talk: Dialogues (→ p. 27/ex. 5)

a) Du übst mit deinem Partner/deiner Partnerin. Zusammen bildet ihr kleine Dialoge.
Sucht euch aus, wer zuerst A and wer zuerst B beginnt. Später könnt ihr die Rollen tauschen.

Example:
A: I really like your shoes.
B: Thanks. I bought them yesterday. – How was your trip to the zoo?
A: It was great! I saw a lot of beautiful animals.

A

Partner B starts with these ideas and then listens to Partner A's answers:

When Partner A starts, Partner B looks for the correct picture and then gives the answer.

I really like your _____ .

Yes, it came this morning.

Hey, where's your _____ ?

Yes, my parents gave it to me for my birthday.

Was the _____ good?

Sorry, I was hungry. So I ate them all.

Let's go to the Science _____ .

It fell out of my pocket and now it doesn't work.

Why does it always _____ on Sunday?

It was great! I saw a lot of beautiful animals.

B

Partner B starts with these ideas and then listens to Partner A's answers:

How was your trip to the _____ ?

Oh, there are no _____ in the cupboard.

Is that _____ for me?

I see you've got a new _____ .

What's the problem with your _____ ?

When Partner A starts, Partner B looks for the correct picture and then gives the answer.

Oh no! I left it on the bus.

No, I went there last weekend.

Thanks. I bought them yesterday.

It doesn't always rain. Last Sunday was nice and sunny.

Yes, it was a fantastic game.

b) *Make different dialogues. Change the ideas in the pictures or change the answers.*

2 Language

19 What happened to Terry's hair? (→ p. 28/ex. 1)
Correct the sentences.

1. On Tuesday Terry arrived late for school. – On Wednesday Terry arrived late for school.
2. He wanted his hair green. – He wanted his hair blond.
3. He dyed his hair six times. – He washed his hair six times.
4. He asked his parents for a wig. – He asked his parents for a sick note.
5. His mum said, "Yes." – His mum said, "No!"
6. His dad looked very angry. – His dad laughed.

20 Fun after school yesterday (→ p. 28/ex. 1)

a) *Read what Lisa says. Find the right verbs and make the past forms.*

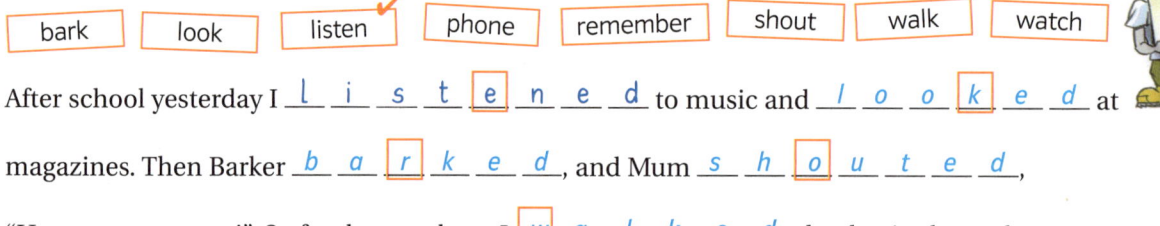

bark | look | listen ✓ | phone | remember | shout | walk | watch

After school yesterday I **listened** to music and **looked** at magazines. Then Barker **barked**, and Mum **shouted**, "He wants to go out!". So for the next hour I **walked** the dog in the park. After tea my friend Emma **phoned** me for a chat. Then it was time for 'Eastenders', so I **watched** TV. It was a great evening. But then suddenly I **remembered** what I sometimes forget to do!

b) *What does Lisa sometimes forget to do? Make the word with the letters in the boxes in a).*

She sometimes forgets to do her **homework**.

21 At the ice rink (→ p. 28/ex. 2)

Complete the text with the correct past forms.

Last Saturday Emma, Lisa, Terry and Sam (go) **went** to the ice rink. There (be) **were** a lot of kids on the ice, but Emma (look) **looked** a bit scared. "Hm. Do we really want to try this?" she (ask) **asked**. "Yes," (answer) **answered** Terry. He (try) **tried** first, but he (fall) **fell** on his face. Lisa (laugh) **laughed**. "Watch, Terry! This is how you do it!" she (shout) **shouted**. But soon she (be) **was** on her face, too. Sam also (have) **had** problems. Only Emma (find) **found** it easy. I'm really happy we (come) **came** to the ice rink," she (smile) **smiled**.

> Is the verb regular or irregular? Not sure? Look at the list on page 203 in your book.

22 Thank you (→ p. 31/ex. 3)

a) *Read the story.*

On Monday after school Sam and his friends Terry, Lisa and Emma were in Greenwich Park. They had a ball and Lisa threw it to Sam. But he was a bit slow and the ball went behind a tree. When Sam ran after the ball he soon found it. But he also found a wallet[1] behind the tree. He showed the wallet to the others and Terry opened it. They were all really excited because there was a lot of money in it – over one hundred pounds!

For the next two or three minutes they laughed and talked about how to spend the money. Terry's idea was a long trip on the Thames, Emma's idea was to buy clothes at Harrods, and Lisa and Sam wanted to have a big party for all their friends. But of course it wasn't their money, so they soon stopped their crazy ideas. There was no name or address in the wallet, so they took it to the police and left it there.

On Tuesday after school a policeman phoned Sam. He wanted to see Sam and his friends again. When they went back the policeman said, "This morning a woman came and asked about the wallet. It fell out of her bag when she was in the park yesterday lunchtime. But she only found out later, and when she went back to the park in the evening her wallet wasn't there. She was very pleased you gave the wallet to the police and she'd like to say thank you. She works at the Arena – so here are four tickets for you for the big ice hockey game next Saturday!"

b) *How can Sam tell his mother what happened? Put the words in the right order.*

1. were • my friends • On Monday after school • and I • in Greenwich Park

   On Monday after school my friends and I were in Greenwich Park.

2. in it • a wallet • found • We • with a lot of money

   We found a wallet with a lot of money in it.

3. the police • We • the wallet • to • took

   We took the wallet to the police.

4. we've got • four tickets • Now • for the big ice hockey game

   Now we've got four tickets for the big ice hockey game.

23 My Storybook (→ p. 31/ex. 3)   (Lösungsvorschlag S. 86)

a) *Make a little story about what you found. Write your story in your exercise book.*

You can say:
- when it was.
- where you were.
- who was with you.
- what you found.
- where you took it.
- what happened then.

+

last Sunday • yesterday • …
in the street • in a shop • at school …

my friend • my brother • …
a bag/a mobile • a little dog • …

home • to the police • to the address on it • …
…

These ideas can help you. Or you can use different ideas.

b) *Work with your partner. Help each other to check your stories. Are all the words correct?*

[1] wallet ['wɒlɪt] – *Brieftasche, Geldbeutel*

2 Wordwise

24 Numbers (→ p. 32/ex. 1)

How much are these cars? Say the numbers to your partner. Your partner writes them down. Are they correct?

£780,000   £12,420   £99   £5,100,000

25 Lisa phones Emma (→ p. 32/ex. 4)

Put in: in – at – on

Lisa: Hi, Emma. Are you _at_ home?

Emma: Yes, I'm _in_ my room. I'm just putting a new poster _on_ the wall. Where are you?

Lisa: I'm _at_ a bus stop _in_ Church Street. I'm _on_ my way to your house!

26 Make six words (→ p. 32/ex. 4)

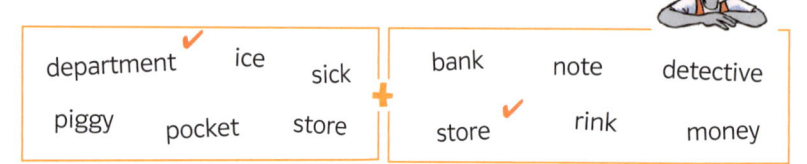

department ✓ | ice | sick | bank | note | detective
piggy | pocket | store | store ✓ | rink | money

1. department store
2. piggy bank
3. sick note
4. store detective
5. pocket money
6. ice rink

27 What are they saying? (→ p. 32/ex. 4)

I'm | lucky | bored | cold | in a hurry

I'm not interested in these things.
I'm _bored._

Close the window, please.
I'm _cold._

I dropped it but it isn't broken.
I'm _lucky._

Sorry, I can't stop and talk.
I'm _in a hurry._

28 Complete the dialogue with the correct forms (→ p. 33/ex. 1)

Sam: I phoned you yesterday, Lisa, but you __weren't__ at home.

Where __were__ you? With Emma?

Lisa: No, I __was__ with my brother Ben.

We __were__ at the Science Museum.

Sam: __Was__ it your first time there?

Lisa: Yes, it __was__. Sometimes I find museums boring, but I __wasn't__ bored yesterday. The planes in the Flight Lab __were__ great!

(was wasn't / were weren't)

29 The party (→ p. 33/ex. 2)

Two friends had a party last Saturday. Read what they said before the party.
Then write about the party.

1. "We can *invite* lots of friends."
2. "Let's *buy* nice drinks."
3. "And let's *make* sandwiches."
4. "We can *play* music at the party."
5. "Of course. Then we can *dance*."
6. "Let's *organize* some games."
7. "Let's *watch* funny videos, too."
8. "I'm sure we can *have* a lot of fun!"

1. __They invited a lot of friends.__
2. __They bought nice drinks.__
3. __They made sandwiches.__
4. __They played music.__
5. __They danced.__
6. __They organized games.__
7. __They watched funny videos.__
8. __They had a lot of fun.__

30 Last Sunday (→ p. 33/ex. 3)

Look at the pictures and write down what happened last Sunday.

1: go into
2: put on • laugh
3: sit down • look at
4: be not pleased
5: take • leave

1. Last Sunday two girls __went into a department store.__
2. First they __put on hats__ and __laughed.__
3. Then they __sat down__ and __looked at magazines.__
4. But the store detective __wasn't pleased.__
5. He __took the girls__ and they __left the department store.__

Revision 1

1 On the school bus (→ p. 34/ex. 2)

Put in the right form. Use the simple present or the present progressive.

1. We _are doing_ (*do*) a project in French at the moment. What about you?

2. At the moment we _are learning_ (*learn*) songs. We often _sing_ (*sing*) songs in French.

3. Look! That boy over there _is looking_ (*look*) at you! Do you know why?

4. Oh, he _does_ (*do*) that every day.

5. Look, that silly dog _is running_ (*run*) after the bus.

6. Yes, it _does_ (*do*) that every morning.

7. Look, my sister _is talking_ (*talk*) to a boy. Who _is_ (*is*) it?

8. I think it _is_ (*be*) Mark. She _meets_ (*meet*) him every morning.

2 Lisa alone at home? (→ p. 35/ex. 3)

Lisa and Terry are walking to the club. They are talking about yesterday.
Complete the dialogue. Use 'was' and 'were'.

Terry: You _were_ n't at the club on Tuesday. Where _were_ you, Lisa?

Lisa: Oh, I _was_ at home in the afternoon.

Terry: And _was_ your brother at home, too?

Lisa: No, he _was_ at a friend's house.

Terry: And where _were_ your parents? _Were_ they at home, too?

Lisa: No, they _were_ in town with Jade.

Terry: So you _were_ alone?

Lisa: No, I _was_ n't.

Terry: You _were_ n't?

Lisa: Barker _was_ with me!

Unit 3   We all need friends!

1 Susan, Jake, Roger or Nicole? (→ p. 37/ex. 1)

Who is speaking?

1. Debbie hated me because I was good at hockey.
   Nicole

2. The kids laughed at my Scottish accent.
   Susan

3. Two boys tried to take my money.
   Jake

4. Bullies laughed at me because I am very small. _Roger_

5. No one played with me at lunchtime. _Susan_

6. After she hit me in a game, I went to hospital. _Nicole_

7. The bullies were surprised because my cousin Todd is really tall. _Roger_

8. I told my dad about the boys, and he talked to my teacher. _Jake_

2 Rhyme time (→ p. 37/ex. 1)

Make words from the letters and say the rhymes.

1. The kids _laugh_ _at_ (glauh ta) me, and I often _cry_ (ycr).

   They don't play with me, and I can't say why.

2. I'm _Scottish_ (soSthcti), and so, you see,

   my _accent_ (tacnec) is strange, but not for me.

3. Some kids are small, and some are _tall_ (lalt).

   But games are there for us all.

4. I came to school late _one_ _day_ (eon yda).

   A _bully_ (lyblu) tried to _hit_ (thi) me, but I said, "Go away!"

5. _Once_ (nOec) my dog _pushed_ (spedhu) me _off_ (ffo) my bed.

   I fell and shouted because I _hit_ (tih) my _head_ (dahe).

twenty-seven 27

3 Let's listen: 'Friends' last night (→ p. 37/ex. 3)

Read the sentences and make a ✔ for 'yes' and a ✘ for 'no'.

1. Phoebe met Mario. ✔
2. Monica and Rachel liked Mario. ✘
3. Mario had a lot of money and lived in a big house. ✘
4. Mario was Italian. ✔
5. Ross and Chandler made pizzas at Carlo's Italian restaurant. ✘
6. Mario lived in a small flat near the restaurant. ✔
7. Joey was really famous in Italy. ✘
8. Joey brought a big pizza from Carlo's. ✔

4 SKILLS: How to write a letter (→ p. 37/ex. 2)   *(individuelle Schülerlösung)*

a) Look at the pictures and read the letters.
b) Choose Tim or Susan as your penfriend and answer his or her letter.
   Write your letter in your exercise book. Say who you are, where you live and what you like.

Hi!

How are you?

My name is Susan and I'm 11 years old. I live in Bristol with my parents and my sister Laura.

I like animals and I've got a cat. Her name is Kitty and she's red, brown and white. I also want a dog for my birthday but Kitty doesn't like dogs.

I like films and I go to the sports club every Saturday. I also like Geography at school but I don't like Maths.

Love,

Susan

Hi!

How are you?

My name is Tim and I'm 12 years old. I live in London with my father and my two brothers, Ben and Peter. Ben is 14 and Peter is 18 years old. I like sport and I play football every day. On Fridays I play basketball with my brother Ben. I've got a dog and his name is Jack.

I like books and I read a comic every week. But I don't like school and I hate homework.

Love,

Tim

5 Last Friday (→ p. 38/ex. 1)

Read the story on page 38. What happened first? What happened then? What happened after that?

- [5] Jake didn't get home before ten.
- [7] Jake took Terry to his room.
- [6] The next day Terry went to Jake's house.
- [2] The message was: "meet u at the youth club at 7".
- [8] Jake said: "Don't tell the others. I have a problem with Maths."
- [1] Terry sent Jake a text message at six o'clock.
- [4] Lisa and Jake did Jake's Maths homework.
- [3] Terry went to the club.

6 A lot of questions (→ p. 38/ex. 2)

a) Read the story on page 38 again. Write answers to the questions. Use 'did' or 'didn't'.

1. Did Jake send Terry a text message? _No, he didn't._
2. Did Terry go to the club? _Yes, he did._
3. Did Jake have supper at the club? _No, he didn't._
4. Did Terry go to Jake's house the next day? _Yes, he did._
5. Did Lisa go to the club? _No, she didn't._
6. Did Lisa invite Jake to supper? _Yes, she did._
7. Did Jake get home before 10? _No, he didn't._
8. Did Lisa and Jake do Jake's Maths homework? _Yes, they did._

b) Some answers in part a) start with 'no'. Write the correct answers in your exercise book. *(Lösungen S. 86)*

7 Last week (→ p. 38/ex. 2)

Look at the pictures and ask Tom what he did last week.

1. watch  — _Did you watch TV?_
2. buy — _Did you buy apples?_
3. read — _Did you read comics?_
4. listen to — _Did you listen to music?_
5. eat — _Did you eat cheese?_
6. play — _Did you play cards?_

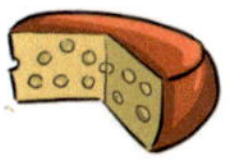

3 — Language

8 Lisa's day (→ p. 39/ex. 3)

a) *Look at the list and read what Lisa did on Saturday.*

b) *Now compare the list with the pictures and write down what she did or didn't do.*

Saturday
feed Barker ✓
draw a picture ✓
pick flowers for Mum ✓

1. Lisa drew a picture.
2. Lisa didn't send a text message.
3. Lisa picked flowers for Mum.
4. Lisa didn't play football.
5. Lisa didn't write a letter.
6. Lisa fed Barker.

1 draw 2 send 3 pick 4 play 5 write 6 feed

9 How did you do that? (→ p. 40)

Read the text on page 40 and match the parts of the sentences.

1. Sam borrowed his dad's bike — a. before his dad bought it.
2. When Sam fell off the bike, — d. he hurt his arm and his face.
3. Terry and Sam put — h. the chain back on the bike.
4. The boys cleaned the bike — f. but there were still black marks on it.
5. Terry found some yellow paint; — g. and tried a trick in the park.
6. Sam's dad took him to the doctor, — b. and she checked his eyes, his ears, and his arm.
7. Sam's dad rode the bike and after that — c. soon the bike looked like new.
8. There were marks on the bike — e. grandma saw yellow marks on his trousers.

10 An interview (→ p. 41/ex. 1)

Read what the famous actor Orlando Bloom said in an interview. What questions did the reporter ask him?

I broke my back because I fell out of a window.
My first film was *The Lord of the Rings*.
When I was young I was in an English TV show.
My Drama teacher gave me roles in school plays.
When I was young I liked sports and girls.
I wore a blond wig in *The Lord of the Rings*.

How? What? Who? When?

1. How did you break your back?
2. What was your first film?
3. When were you in an English TV show?
4. Who gave you roles in school plays?
5. What did you like when you were young?
6. When did you wear a blond wig?

11 Let's talk: On the phone (→ p. 41/ex. 2)

Partner A reads Part A; Partner B reads Part B. Answer the questions, but don't look at your partner's part of the page. Partner A starts.

A

Make questions and check your partner's answers.

**I tried to phone you yesterday
Where were you?**

(Sorry. I was in hospital.)
why?

(I fell off my bike.)
break • arm?

(No, I didn't. But I broke my leg.)
how • happen?

(I tried a trick on my bike.)
where?

(I tried it in the park.)
go • to doctor?

(Yes, I did.)
head • hurt?

(Yes, it did.)
stay • in bed!

B

Check your partner's questions and answer them. Look at the pictures.

(I tried to phone you yesterday. Where were you?)

(Why were you in hospital?)

(Did you break your arm?)

(How did it happen?)

(Where did you try it?)

(Did you go to a doctor?)

(Did your head hurt?)

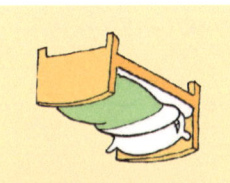

(Then you must stay in bed!)

3 — Language

12 Let's listen: Parts of the body (→ p. 41/ex. 3)

The words are in the box (→ ↓ ↘).

a) Find words for the parts of the body in this puzzle.

S	S	R	Z	R	J	K	N	E	E	S	J
G	N	T	T	F	K	L	A	P	F	L	D
H	O	B	O	E	E	V	M	N	G	E	U
K	S	J	E	M	L	Y	Z	R	B	E	H
G	E	K	S	H	A	K	E	D	N	F	S
T	R	F	W	H	E	C	D	S	M	B	J
F	J	E	S	D	P	A	H	I	J	A	R
G	K	Z	R	L	C	G	M	F	A	C	E
N	F	I	E	A	R	S	T	D	W	K	O
B	O	V	E	E	H	P	X	Z	Q	E	I

b) Read the text and put in the right parts of the body. Then read the sentences again and point to the right part of your body.

1. I open my __eyes__ and what do I see?
   A great, big tiger looking at me.

2. I cover¹ my __ears__ when they start to shout.
   I hope they soon can sort it out!

3. When I go the zoo, I hold² my __nose__.
   Animals don't wash or change their clothes.

4. We leave tonight. Did you pack?
   All I have is on my __back__.

5. The soap is never in its place
   when I want to wash my __face__.

6. I ate too much. Please, don't get mad!
   My __stomach__ hurts. I'm feeling bad.

7. When I wear my shorts, you see my __knees__.
   They look a bit funny, but don't laugh, please.

8. On each foot I have five __toes__.
   Why is that? No one knows.

13 Let's listen: Tom's day (→ p. 41/ex. 3)   (HV-Text S. 86)

How was Tom's day? Find the words.

1. When Tom woke up, his __head__ hurt.
2. When he washed his face, some water got into his __mouth__.
3. When he came into the living room, he hit his __elbow__ on a chair.
4. The books fell off the chair and hurt Tom's __toes__.
5. It was sunny, so Tom closed his __eyes__.
6. He could hear the cat with his big __ears__.
7. Tom fell and hit his __leg__.

¹to cover [ˈkʌvə] – hier: zuhalten; ²to hold [həʊld] – hier: zuhalten

14 Who or which? (→ p. 42/ex. 1)

1. Jake has a good friend from Australia _who_ visits him every year.
2. Lisa has a dog _which_ always follows her to school.
3. Emma has a big sister _who_ talks on the phone for hours.
4. This year the pupils are acting in a school play _which_ is about animals.
5. Tiger is playing with a purple mouse _which_ Terry bought for her.
6. Mrs Carter is a teacher _who_ reads a lot of books.
7. Sam's grandma paints pictures _which_ she sells at the market.
8. Sam has a new computer _which_ he uses every day.
9. Nasreen often makes scones _which_ Emma gives to her friends.
10. In the Drama Club there are a lot of pupils _who_ can sing and dance.

15 A doctor is a person (→ p. 42/ex. 1)

Match the sentence parts and use 'who' or 'which'.

1. A doctor is a person 2. Lisa saw the accident 3. Kids are scared of bullies 4. Jake has a girlfriend 5. Terry found the yellow paint 6. A teacher is a person 7. Pigs are animals 8. Emma has a friend	**+** who which **+**	works in a school and knows things. Sam used on the bike. like apples. works in a hospital and helps people. play tricks on them. lives in Bristol. has a Scottish accent. happened in the park.

1. _A doctor is a person who works in a hospital and helps people._
2. _Lisa saw the accident which happened in the park._
3. _Kids are scared of bullies who play tricks on them._
4. _Jake has a girlfriend who has a Scottish accent._
5. _Terry found the yellow paint which Sam used on the bike._
6. _A teacher is a person who works in a school and knows things._
7. _Pigs are animals which like apples._
8. _Emma has a friend who lives in Bristol._

16 The girl detectives (→ p. 45/ex. 2)

a) *Read the story and then answer the questions.*

Kate and Laura were friends. They often did their homework together. Kate was good at Maths and Laura was good at Science. One day Fiona asked them for help.
"Look," she said. "Here are notes which I found on my books and text messages which I found on my mobile. I'm scared."

"What do they say?" asked Kate. "They're horrible," said Fiona. "This one says: 'We hate you. Take your Scottish accent and go away.'" Laura had an idea. "Kate," she said. "Let's be girl detectives. You can watch Fiona's books and I can watch pupils who are sending text messages."

It worked. The next day Kate and Laura went to the bullies and said, "We know who you are. Stop! You are making Fiona unhappy. We can tell the teacher and Fiona's parents."
Fiona didn't get messages from these bullies again.

Then one day Lisa asked for help. "I can't find Barker," she said. "He followed me to school, but then he ran away." Kate asked, "Where do you walk your dog?" Kate and Laura made a map. They walked from Lisa's house to school and then to the park. They also walked to the cinema and to the supermarket. There was Barker! He was at the door. When he barked people gave him food.

Another day Mrs Carter said, "I can't find my mobile." Kate and Laura found it an hour later. It was …

1. Who did Kate and Laura stop?

    Kate and Laura stopped the bullies.

2. What did the bullies do?

    The bullies wrote notes and text messages.

3. Where was Barker?

    Barker was at the supermarket.

4. Where was Mrs Carter's mobile? What do you think?

    (individuelle Schülerlösung)

b) *Read the story again and look at the pictures. Why are they wrong?*   (Lösungsvorschlag S. 86)

17 My Storybook (→ p. 45/ex. 3)

Write a story about how Kate and Laura found Mrs Carter's mobile. Write in your exercise book.   *(individuelle Schülerlösung)*

18 SKILLS: Looking up words (→ p. 46/ex. 2)

Salami pizza

pizza dough
1 tablespoon of olive oil
1 cup of tinned tomatoes
1 cup of grated cheese
1 chopped onion
12 slices of salami
1 teaspoon of oregano
½ teaspoon of salt
¼ teaspoon of pepper

The red words are like German words.

Look up the blue words in your dictionary.

Heat the oven to 250° C. Grease an oven tray with the olive oil. Roll out the pizza dough and put it on the tray. Spread the tomatoes over the pizza dough. Spread the cheese, the chopped onion and the slices of salami over the tomatoes. Add the oregano, salt and pepper. Put the tray into the oven and bake for 15–20 minutes.

a) *Read the recipe and look at the red and blue words. The red words are like German words. Do you know what they mean? Write the German word next to the English word.*

salami = *Salami* oregano = *Oregano*

olive = *Olive*

b) *Look up the blue words in your dictionary and write down the right meaning.*

dough = *Teig* teaspoon = *Teelöffel*

tablespoon = *Esslöffel* salt = *Salz*

oil = *Öl* pepper = *Pfeffer*

cup = *Tasse* to heat = *erhitzen*

tin = *Dose* to grease = *einölen*

to grate = *reiben* tray = *Blech*

to chop = *hacken* to spread = *verteilen*

onion = *Zwiebel* to bake = *backen*

slice = *Scheibe*

Enjoy your meal![1]

[1] Enjoy your meal! [ɪnˈdʒɔɪ jɔː ˌmiːl] – *Guten Appetit!*

3 | Wordwise

19 Look up these words (→ p. 46/ex. 2)

1. also = _auch_
2. chips = _Pommes frites_
3. fast = _schnell_
4. most = _das meiste_
5. bad = _schlecht_
6. hat = _Hut_
7. last = _letzte/letzter/letztes_
8. stall = _Stand_

> Be careful! They look like German words, but they have different meanings.

20 Adopt an animal (→ p. 46/ex. 2) (Lösungen S. 86)

Look at this poster from London Zoo. There are a lot of words which you don't know.
You can understand some of them because they are like German words.
Look up the other words in your dictionary. The tips in the boxes can help you.
Then tell your partner in German what the text is about.

ADOPT AN ANIMAL

Animal *adoption* is an *unforgettable* birthday present for your parents or your friends because *everyone* likes animals. Of course you can adopt an animal for *yourself*, too.

Make your *donation*
You can adopt every animal and you can *donate* £ 20 or more. Everyone who adopts an animal gets:

- 1 ticket to London Zoo
- a photo of the animal
- a *subscription* to „Lifewatch" magazine

The names of the people who adopt an animal are also on a 'thank you' board in the Zoo.

You can find more information and pictures of all the animals which you can adopt on our *website*.

Choose an animal
Choose an animal which you want to adopt, for example:

a *butterfly*, a *camel*, a *cobra*, an *elephant*, a *giraffe*, a *monkey*, a *tiger* or a *zebra*.

> *Adopt* klingt so ähnlich wie das deutsche Wort: … .

> *Adoption* kenne ich aus dem Deutschen: … .

> *Forget* kenne ich. Dann kann *unforgettable* nur … heißen.

> *Everyone* hat etwas mit *every* zu tun.

> *You* kenne ich schon. Also heißt *yourself*: … .

> Schwierig! Das Wort muss ich nachschlagen.

> Also *donation* heißt … . Dann kann *donate* nur … heißen.

> Noch ein schwieriges Wort, das ich nachschlagen muss!

> Die meisten Tiernamen kenne ich aus dem Deutschen. Dann muss ich nur noch *butterfly* und *monkey* nachschlagen.

> Dieses Wort benutzt man auch im Deutschen.

> Das ist bestimmt der Name einer Zeitschrift.

| Check-in | Language | Story | Wordwise | **Check-out** | **3** |

21 No, that's wrong   (→ p. 47/ex. 1)

Correct these sentences.

Example: The bullies gave Jake pocket money. The bullies didn't give Jake pocket money.

1. Nicole hit Debbie on the head in a hockey game. _Nicole didn't hit Debbie on the head in a hockey game._

2. Jake went to the youth club with Terry. _Jake didn't go to the youth club with Terry._

3. Lisa and Jake did their English homework. _Lisa and Jake didn't do their English homework._

22 Did you go to the cinema last night?   (→ p. 47/ex. 2)

Ask questions with 'did'. Answer the questions with 'Yes, … did.' or 'No, … didn't.'

Example: go • the • night • cinema • you • to • last: no
Did you go to the cinema last night? – No, I didn't.

1. kids • at • play • Susan • the • lunchtime • with: no

   Did the kids play with Susan at lunchtime? No, they didn't.

2. Lisa's • Jake • supper • house • at • have: yes

   Did Jake have supper at Lisa's house? Yes, he did.

3. his • Sam • bike • dad's • borrow: yes

   Did Sam borrow his dad's bike? Yes, he did.

4. mark • Maths • really • a • in • good • get • test • Sam • the: no

   Did Sam get a really good mark in the Maths test? No, he didn't.

23 Who or which?   (→ p. 47/ex. 3)

Use 'who' or 'which' and underline the right part of the sentence.

1. At school we are scared of kids _who_ <u>bully other kids</u> • are very small.

2. I can write letters to friends _who_ can't read • <u>aren't at my school.</u>

3. Kids get really good marks in subjects _which_ they think are stupid • <u>they like.</u>

4. I always watch TV shows _which_ <u>are funny</u> • are for old people.

5. Sam is a boy _who_ can't ride a bike • <u>does tricks on his bike.</u>

6. Sam's dad has trousers _which_ are very cheap • <u>have yellow marks on them.</u>

thirty-seven 37

Unit 4 You are what you eat!

1 Good food (→ p. 49/ex. 1)

Put a ✔ in the correct box.

1. You eat takeaway food … .
   ☐ at school ✔ at home ☐ in a café

2. You can get Indian food at … .
   ☐ La Caverna ☐ Ching Ming ✔ the Taj Mahal

3. The food at La Caverna is … .
   ☐ English ✔ Italian ☐ Chinese

4. All of these restaurants are in … .
   ✔ Greenwich ☐ London ☐ Berlin

5. The list of food in a restaurant is on a … .
   ☐ card ☐ book ✔ menu

2 In a restaurant (→ p. 49/ex. 1)

Find the words.

1. You often get … with Chinese food.
2. … is an Italian soup.
3. Lamb curry is very … .
4. You can start your meal with a … .
5. … is an Indian drink.
6. Chinese food often tastes sweet and … .
7. Is … from a cow or a pig? – It's from a pig.
8. You can drink … with your meal.
9. The big part of the meal is the … .
10. In an Indian restaurant you can often eat rice pudding for … .

Crossword answers:
- RICE
- MINESTRONE
- SPICY
- STARTER
- LASSI
- SOUR
- PORK
- MINERAL WATER
- MAIN COURSE
- DESSERT

3 Let's listen: What's for supper? (→ p. 49/ex. 3)

Listen to the text and fill in the correct words.

1. _Grandma_ is still at the doctor's.
2. They can order their food from a _takeaway_.
3. There's a good _Indian restaurant_ near the market.
4. The _Chinese_ restaurant doesn't do takeaways.
5. _Italian food_ is OK for Grandma.
6. They've got great pizzas at _La Caverna_.
7. They have spaghetti and _minestrone_ soup for only three pounds.
8. Mr Spencer's address is _129_ Romney Road.

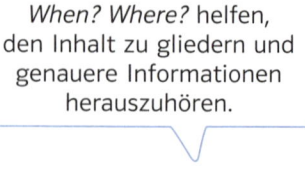

> Fragewörter wie Who? What? Why? When? Where? helfen, den Inhalt zu gliedern und genauere Informationen herauszuhören.

4 That's good! (→ p. 50/ex. 2)

a) *Draw a line to match three pictures. Use different colours.*

b) *Now choose an adjective and compare the things in the pictures.*

big • nice • easy • fast • tasty ✔

1. Apples are tasty. Crisps are tastier than apples. But pizza is the tastiest.

2. Bikes are fast. Buses are faster. But cars are the fastest.

3. Pigs are nice. Cows are nicer. But sheep are the nicest.

4. Maths is easy. English is easier. But German is the easiest.

5. Tents are big. Sheds are bigger. But houses are the biggest.

5 Doggy the dog (→ p. 51/ex. 3)

Doggy the dog compares things he likes and doesn't like.
Look at the pictures and fill in the comparative and superlative forms of 'good' and 'bad'.

1. I think dog food is *good*,

   bread is *better*

   but burgers are *the best*!

2. For me, too much sport is *bad*,

   loud music is *worse*

   but cold tea is *the worst*!

thirty-nine 39

4 Check-in **Language** Story Wordwise Check-out

👥 6 Let's compare (→ p. 51/ex. 4)

a) *Compare these people or things and write the words or names in the boxes.*
b) *Now use the adjective and the comparative form of this adjective and make sentences.*
c) *Read the sentences to your partner.*

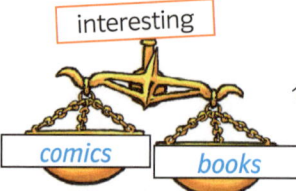

interesting
comics / books

1. Books are interesting, but comics are more interesting.

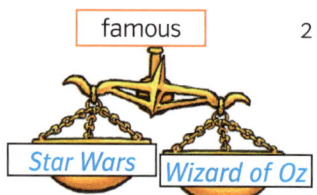

famous
Star Wars / Wizard of Oz

2. "The Wizard of Oz" is famous, but "Star Wars" is more famous.

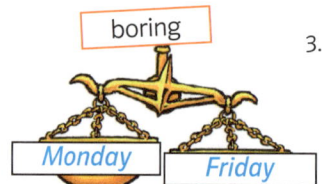

boring
Monday / Friday

3. Fridays are boring, but Mondays are more boring.

beautiful
hat / wig

4. Wigs are beautiful, but hats are more beautiful.

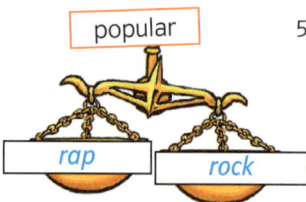

popular
rap / rock

5. Rock music is popular, but rap music is more popular.

7 Food adjectives (→ p. 51/ex. 4)

Write down the comparative and superlative forms of the adjectives.

healthy	healthier	the healthiest
spicy	spicier	the spiciest
exciting	more exciting	the most exciting
sweet	sweeter	the sweetest
tasty	tastier	the tastiest
expensive	more expensive	the most expensive

8 Emma's dream boyfriend (→ p. 52/ex. 1)

Emma dreams that she has got a boyfriend who does everything for her. Look at her dream and write down what she needn't do because her boyfriend does it for her.

1. She needn't do her homework.
2. She needn't help her mum.
3. She needn't wash the car.
4. She needn't write the Maths test.
5. She needn't buy milk.
6. She needn't make sandwiches.
7. She needn't pick flowers.
8. She needn't finish the History project.

1. do my homework
2. help my mum
3. wash the car
4. write the Maths test
5. buy milk
6. make sandwiches
7. pick flowers
8. finish the History project

9 Tom's rules (→ p. 52/ex. 1)

The Jacksons are on a camping trip in Italy. Tiger must stay at home and Tom is looking after her. He tells her what she must or mustn't do. Look what Tom says and complete the sentences.

1. You must eat cat food.
2. You mustn't eat mice.
3. You must stay in the garden.
4. You mustn't sit in front of my door.
5. You must sleep in your bed in the kitchen.
6. You mustn't sleep in Terry's bed.
7. You must drink water.
8. You mustn't drink my milk.
9. You must play with your ball.
10. You mustn't play with real mice.
11. And you mustn't bring other cats into the house!

10 Must or needn't (→ p. 52/ex. 1)

Complete the sentences with ‚must' or ‚needn't'.

I _needn't_ go on a diet. I'm already fit.

We _must_ help you with your diet.

But you _needn't_ watch me every minute of the day.

But you _must_ watch what you eat.

I _needn't_ exercise. I play football every day.

But you _must_ drink a lot of water.

You _must_ eat breakfast before school.

But I _needn't_ eat all of it. It's too much!

11 What to do (→ p. 53/ex. 3)

Betty, the new girl in your class, always asks you when she has got a problem. You are nice and tell her what she should do. The words in boxes can help you.

| eat a sandwich ✓ | ask your mum | wear a pullover | buy a new T-shirt | go to a doctor | invite your friends |

1. She is hungry. — You should eat a sandwich.
2. She doesn't like her old T-shirt. — You should buy a new T-shirt.
3. She is cold. — You should wear a pullover.
4. She has got a strange mark on the nose. — You should go to a doctor.
5. She wants to have a party. — You should invite your friends.
6. She needs money. — You should ask your mum.

| Check-in | **Language** | Story | Wordwise | Check-out | **4** |

✿ 12 A healthy school (→ p. 53/ex. 3)

Look at the pictures and make questions with the words. Then write an answer.

1 
drink • you • the • cafeteria • mustn't • what • in?

What mustn't you drink in the cafeteria?

You mustn't drink coke.

_____

2 
where • shouldn't • skate • you?

Where shouldn't you skate?

You shouldn't skate in the playground.

_____

3 
you • bring • needn't • fruit • why • from • home?

Why needn't you bring fruit from home?

You can buy fruit in the cafeteria.

_____

4

	Wednesday
8:10 – 9:00	English
9:10 – 10:00	Math
10:10 – 11:00	German
11:10 – 12:00	Science
13:10 – 15:10	PE (Sport)

go • sport • when • must • you • to • on • Wednesdays?

When must you go to sport on Wednesdays?

You must go to sport at 13:10.

_____

✿ ◉ 13 Let's listen: Five times a day (→ p. 53/ex. 5)   (HV-Text S.87)

Listen to the text. The pupils are asking Dr Bell some more questions in Science class. Are these sentences right ✔ or wrong ✘ ?

1. You should eat fruit and vegetables five times a day. ✔
2. Dr Bell says one glass of juice[1] once a day is OK. ✔
3. Lemonade is not real juice. ✔
4. You must only eat fruit and vegetables for meals. ✘
6. Fruit is better. ✘
7. Terry only likes apples. ✔
8. You should like all fruit and vegetables. ✘

[1] juice [dʒuːs] – *Saft*

forty-three 43

4 | Check-in | **Language** | Story | Wordwise | Check-out

14 Let's talk: Talking to the class (→ p. 53/ex. 5)

a) *You and your partner are telling the class about food and exercise, but your notes are mixed up¹. Put the sentences in the right order and read them to the class. Partner A starts.*

A	B
5 Breakfast is the first meal of the day.	10 Fruit is a good breakfast food.
9 But you should eat the right food.	6 It helps you to get a good start.
1 Good morning.	4 The first questions is: What did you eat for breakfast this morning?
11 And some cornflakes.	12 Now you can plan a healthy breakfast for tomorrow morning.
3 Are you ready to begin?	2 Today we are talking about food and exercise.
7 That's why you should never leave the house without breakfast.	8 You needn't eat a big breakfast.

b) *Now use the ideas in the grid. Write your own text and read it to the class.*

A	B
next • talk about • exercise	needn't • exercise • every day
3 or 4 times • a week • good	needn't • exercise • long
30 minutes • OK	should • try • different sports
must • find • sport • which you like	mustn't • be • too difficult
then • can • have fun	and • get fit • too

Next we are talking about exercise. You should try different sports. You must find a sport which you like.

It mustn't be too difficult. You needn't exercise every day. 3 or 4 times a week is good. You needn't

exercise long. 30 minutes is OK. Then you can have fun and get fit, too.

¹ mixed up [ˌmɪkst ˈʌp] – *durcheinander*

15 Time for lunch (→ p. 54/ex. 1)

a) *Lisa and Jade must make their lunch today. Look at the picture and write sentences.*

They've got some chips.   They haven't got any milk.

They've got some peas.   They haven't got any bread.

They've got some tomatoes.   They haven't got any sausages.

They've got some lettuce.   They haven't got any cheese.

They've got some beans.   They haven't got any oranges.

b) *Write sentences about what they can't make for lunch.*

1. They can't make pizza because they haven't got any cheese.

2. They can't make sandwiches because they haven't got any bread.

3. They can't make sausages and chips because they haven't got any sausages.

c) *What do you think Lisa and Jade make for lunch? Why? Write in your exercise book.* (Lösungsvorschlag S. 86)

16 What can I drink? (→ p. 54/ex. 3)

Fill in 'some' or 'any'.

Emma: Have you got _any_ milk?

Mum: No, but I've got _some_ coke.

Emma: I don't want _any_ coke.

Mum: You can have _some_ lassi.

Emma: No, I think I want _some_ mineral water.

Mum: I'm sorry. I haven't got _any_ water. But I can give you _some_ tea.

Emma: OK. Can I have _some_ milk in my tea?

17 Grant's big race (→ p. 57/ex. 4)

Look at the pictures and complete the sentences.

1. On Monday Grant and __Terry__ are looking at a __poster__. There is a __school race__ on __Saturday__ and Grant __wants to win__.

2. Later Grant is in __the park__. He is exercising for __the race__. Suddenly he sees a big __poster__. It says: __Eat spaghetti!__

3. Every day Grant eats __spaghetti__. He eats it for __breakfast__, for __lunch__ and for __supper__. The problem is: Spaghetti isn't tasty any more[1] …

4. On __Saturday__ the race starts at __ten o'clock__. Grant starts the race very fast but then he feels __sick__. At the end of the race, he is the __slowest__ runner.

5. After the race all the runners __eat__ __spaghetti__. But Grant __doesn't eat spaghetti__. He doesn't like spaghetti any more.

[1] not … any more [ˌeni ˈmɔː] – *nicht mehr*

18 Wrong word (→ p. 58/ex. 1)

Which word in these groups is different? Underline it. Find a group word for each group.

1. <u>pea</u> • pear • orange • apple: _fruit_
2. pudding • cake • <u>lassi</u> • ice-cream: _dessert_
3. <u>snack</u> • breakfast • lunch • dinner: _meal_
4. jogging • swimming • running • <u>eating</u>: _sport_
5. bird • mouse • dog • <u>shop</u>: _animal_
6. pea • <u>pear</u> • lettuce • bean: _vegetable_

19 Restaurant jokes (→ p. 58/ex. 3)

Complete the jokes. Use the words in the box.

| soup | food | dessert | cheese |
| waiters | eating | hot | laughing |

1. Waiter, this _dessert_ looks funny.

   Then why aren't you _laughing_ ?

2. What's this mouse doing in my _cheese_ ?

   It looks like it's _eating_ it.

3. The _waiters_ here are terrible.

   You think they're terrible? Wait until you see the _food_ !

4. Waiter, your finger is in my _soup_ .

   Don't worry. It's not _hot_ .

20 Meals (→ p. 58/ex. 3)

Complete the mind map and write down the different meals of the day.
Then tell your partner what you can have for these meals.

(individuelle Schülerlösung)

- breakfast
- tea
- meals
- lunch
- supper

21 Comparison of adjectives (→ p. 59/ex. 1)

Do you remember the rule for the comparison of adjectives?
Write the comparative and superlative forms of these adjectives.

1. fit — fitter — the fittest
2. dangerous — more dangerous — the most dangerous
3. healthy — healthier — the healthiest
4. fresh — fresher — the freshest
5. unhealthy — more unhealthy — the most unhealthy

22 Which modal verb is it? (→ p. 59/ex. 2)

Underline the correct forms.

1. We must • **mustn't** eat on the sports field.
2. We mustn't • **needn't** take our books home every day. We have lockers.
3. We **must** • shouldn't eat between 12:00 and 13:00. After 13:00 the cafeteria closes.
4. You **shouldn't** • needn't eat so many sweets. They're bad for you.
5. You **must** • mustn't drink more water. It's healthier for you.

23 Some and any (→ p. 59/ex. 3)

Write the questions and answers in English.

1. Frage, ob der Verkäufer heute Karotten hat. – Er sagt, dass er keine hat, aber er hat Tomaten.

   Have you got any carrots today?

   I haven't got any carrots but I've got some tomatoes.

2. Frage den Kellner, ob er heute Obstsalat hat. – Er sagt, dass er welchen hat.

   Have you got any fruit salad today?

   Yes, I've got some.

3. Frage deine Lehrerin, ob sie heute Hausaufgaben für euch hat. – Sie sagt, dass sie welche hat, die aber sehr einfach sind.

   Have you got any homework for us today?

   Yes, I've got some, but it's very easy.

Revision 2   R

1 Tina's Party (→ p. 60/ex. 1)

a) *Last Saturday Tina had a party with her friends. Read the text and look at the picture. Say what Tina did and didn't do.*

Last Saturday Tina __had__ (*have*) a party but she __didn't invite__ (*invite*) any girls. She only __invited__ (*invite*) her friends Bill, Bob and Tony. Tina __was__ (*be*) very excited so she __did__ (*do*) some strange things. She __put__ (*put*) some glasses on the table but then she __put__ (*put*) the apples in the glasses. She __made__ (*make*) a cake and some sandwiches but she __didn't bring__ (*bring*) any plates. She __put__ (*put*) the sandwiches in the hat and the fish in the oven. She __bought__ (*buy*) some crisps and some bananas, but her friends __didn't find__ (*find*) them because they __were__ (*be*) on the cupboard. She __didn't wear__ (*wear*) her new shoes but she __wore__ (*wear*) her new T-shirt. Tina __was__ (*be*) happy because she __looked__ (*look*) very beautiful.

b) *Compare Tina's boyfriends. Use 'tall', 'old' and 'happy'.*

1. __Bill is taller than Bob__, but __Tony is the tallest.__
2. __Bill is older than Tony, but Bob is the oldest.__
3. __Bob is happier than Tony, but Bill is the happiest.__

forty-nine 49

Meine Lernbiografie 3

Jetzt hast du schon vier Units bearbeitet. Es wird wieder einmal Zeit, über das Lernen nachzudenken. Das kennst du ja noch vom letzten Jahr. Fülle also bitte die Tabelle aus. Denke gut nach und frage deinen Lehrer/deine Lehrerin, wenn du dir nicht sicher bist.

Was ich jetzt alles kann!

Trage den entsprechenden Smiley in der entsprechenden Farbe ein.

		Kann ich super.	Das klappt meistens.	Das ist nicht so einfach.
Hören	Ich kann verstehen, was im Unterricht gesagt und gefragt wird.			
	Ich kann Arbeitsanweisungen meines Lehrers/meiner Lehrerin und von einer CD verstehen und darauf reagieren.			
	Ich verstehe auch längere Hörtexte und kann zusammenfassen, worum es darin geht.			
	Ich kann Hörtexten auch einzelne Informationen entnehmen und Fragen zum Gehörten beantworten.			
Hören und Sehen	Ich kann Filme und Videoclips verstehen und zusammenfassen, worum es geht.			
	Ich kann Fragen zu einzelnen Informationen aus Filmen und Videoclips beantworten.			
Sprechen	Ich kann mich am Unterrichtsgespräch beteiligen.			
	Ich kann mich vorstellen, jemanden grüßen oder mich verabreden.			
	Ich kann jemanden einladen und auf Einladungen reagieren.			
	Ich kann mich an Gesprächen beteiligen, in denen es um Alltag, Schule, Freizeit und Freundschaft geht.			
	Ich kann mich in Alltagssituationen verständlich machen, z.B. bei einer Wegbeschreibung, in Restaurants, in Geschäften und in öffentlichen Verkehrsmitteln.			
	Ich kann einfache Geschichten nacherzählen.			
	Ich kann über ein wichtiges Erlebnis berichten.			
	Ich kann Personen, Gegenstände oder Ereignisse mit einfachen Sätzen beschreiben.			
	Ich kann Arbeitsergebnisse kurz und zusammenhängend präsentieren, wenn ich mich darauf vorbereitet habe.			

Lernbiografie L

Lesen	Ich kann alle Arbeitsanweisungen in meinen Englischmaterialien verstehen und entsprechend darauf reagieren.			
	Ich kann unterschiedliche Texte selbstständig lesen und das Wichtigste verstehen.			
	Ich kann auch längere Geschichten lesen und verstehen.			
	Ich kann Einzelheiten aus Texten herausfinden und Aufgaben dazu lösen.			
	Ich kann Geschichten, Gedichte und andere Texte ausdrucksvoll laut vorlesen.			
Schreiben	Ich kann einen Notizzettel schreiben, um jemanden zu informieren.			
	Ich kann Postkarten, einen einfachen persönlichen Brief oder E-Mails schreiben.			
	Ich kann einfache kürzere Texte über Erlebtes, Erlesenes oder Erfundenes für meinen *folder* schreiben.			

Was ich noch besser machen kann!

> Sehr gut! Nun hast du herausgefunden, was du besonders gut kannst und woran du noch arbeiten solltest. Dabei kann dir ein Lernplan helfen. Schreibe auf, woran du in nächster Zeit arbeiten willst.

Daran möchte ich noch arbeiten:

_____
_____

Dafür werde ich folgendes tun:

_____
_____

Tipps von meinem Lehrer/meiner Lehrerin:

_____
_____

Datum: _____ Unterschrift: _____

> Super! Nach Unit 7 schauen wir, ob du deine Ziele erreicht hast.

fifty-one 51

Unit 5   Media: music and more!

1 Matching the media   (→ p. 62/ex. 1)

a) *Write down what you can see in the picture.*

b) *What can you do with these things? In some examples there can be more than one answer.*

1. You can _watch films_ with a _DVD player_.
2. You can _take photos_ with a _digital camera_.
3. You can _listen to music_ with an _MP3 player_.

2 Update your grandma!   (→ p. 62/ex. 1)

Terry is showing his grandma his room. She doesn't know much about media. How does he answer her questions?

surf • watch • films • computer • digital • DVD player • MP3

Grandma: Terry, what's a laptop?

Terry: It's a _computer_, Grandma.

Grandma: And what do you do on your laptop?

Terry: I _surf_ the Internet.

Grandma: And what's that over there?

Terry: It's my _DVD player_.

You can _watch_ DVDs with a DVD player, and DVDs are like videos, so you can see _films_ like *Spiderman* or *Star Wars* at home.

Grandma: And is that an M3P player?

Terry: No, it's my _digital_ camera, Grandma. And the word is _MP3_ player.

Grandma: Oh, these things are too difficult for me! I just don't understand them!

3 Let's listen: Terry's new webcam   (→ p. 63/ex. 5)

Terry is talking about his new webcam. Listen. Which of these facts are correct? Make a ✔ for 'yes' and a ✘ for 'no'.

1. Terry has lost his MP3 player. ✔
2. Terry's CD player is new. ✘
3. He has got about 15 DVDs. ✔
4. One of his DVDs is *Matrix*. ✔
5. Terry and Phil have got a *Spiderman* DVD. ✘
6. They did *The Wizard of Oz* at school last month. ✘
7. Terry says *The Wizard of Oz* was fun. ✔
8. Terry never uses his laptop to do his homework. ✔

4 Mixed verb forms (→ p. 65/ex. 1)

a) Put the letters in the correct order.

1. Sam has CPIEOD ten songs. —— _copied_
2. Terry has already RINDPTE the cover. —— _printed_
3. He has EKNAT some good photos. —— _taken_
4. Sam has DUNOF a text about *The Wizard of Oz*. —— _found_
5. Terry and Emma have already ECADT it at school. —— _acted_
6. Emma has EONG to Bristol. —— _gone_

b) Make a grammar card for these verb forms. Start like this: (Lösung S. 86)

infinitive	simple past form	present perfect form
to copy	copied	copied

5 What has Tom done? (→ p. 65/ex. 1)

Look at the pictures and say what Tom has done.

1. _Tom has finished his homework._
2. _Tom has found £ 10._
3. _Tom has left his bag._
4. _Tom has lost his ticket._

5 Language

6 Media (→ p. 65/ex. 2)

Make sentences as in the example. Use the present perfect.

Example: Terry has just decided to buy a new CD player.

1. I **have just downloaded** a fantastic song. (just • download)
2. She **has just borrowed** my MP3 player. (just • borrow)
3. Sam **has already copied** the text for his friends. (already • copy)
4. The *Crazy Cats* **have already recorded** a new song, *Big Bad Tiger*. (already • record)
5. The teacher **has already printed out** the song text for us. (already • print out)
6. I **have just deleted** all my old e-mails. (just • delete)

7 A busy day (→ p. 65/ex. 3)

The Taylors have made lists of all the things which they have done today. What do they say?

- make a chocolate cake ✓
- take photos of Barker ✓
- leave the window open ✓
- do my homework ✓
- find my ball ✓
- eat all my supper 🐾

1. Sue: **I've made a chocolate cake.**
2. Richard: **I've taken photos of Barker.**
3. Ben: **I've left the window open.**
4. Lisa: **I've done my homework.**
5. Jade: **I've found my ball.**
6. Barker: **I've eaten all my supper.**

8 Irregular verbs (→ p. 65/ex. 3)

Find the simple past form (second form) and the present perfect form (third form) of these irregular verbs and write them down.

to take	took	taken
to leave	left	left
to make	made	made
to eat	ate	eaten
to find	found	found
to do	did	done
to go	went	gone
to lose	lost	lost

took	lost	did	found
made	went	taken	ate
lost	left	found	done
eaten	made	gone	left

9 They're all perfect! (→ p. 65/ex. 3)

Mr Taylor is having computer lessons in Bristol. In the evening he phones his family. Fill in the correct English verb forms and use the present perfect.

Mr Taylor: Hi Sue! It's Richard. I've got a problem with the computer. Can I talk to Lisa, please?

Mrs Taylor: Hi Richard! No, sorry. Lisa _has_ just _left_ (*verlassen*) the house. She's visiting Emma.

Mr Taylor: OK, can I talk to Ben then?

Mrs Taylor: No, Ben's not here. He _has gone_ (*gehen*) to a football match. Can I help you?

Mr Taylor: Well, I tried to send you an e-mail but it didn't work. There must be something wrong with our computer.

Mrs Taylor: That's funny. I _have_ just _sent_ (*schicken*) an e-mail to Farah and she _has_ already _answered_ (*antworten*) it.

Mr Taylor: Oh. Maybe there's a problem with my laptop. What's that noise?

Mrs Taylor: Barker _has dropped_ (*fallen lassen*) his ball into his bowl. I must go and clean the kitchen. Lisa can phone you when she's back. Bye, Richard!

10 Who says this? (→ p. 66/text)

Write down the names.

1. Steve Jones has sent me an e-mail about *The Wizard of Oz*. __Emma__
2. Have you ever been to Greenwich Youth Club? __Lisa__
3. Has Mrs Carter sent you an e-mail? __Lisa__
4. Have you two gone bananas? __Emma__
5. You and Terry have sung and danced before. __Lisa__
6. But I haven't done the plan for my story for English yet. __Emma__

11 Emma's e-mail (→ p. 66/ex. 1)

Emma is writing an e-mail to a friend. On the right you can see what she is thinking. What does she write? Use 'Have you … ?'

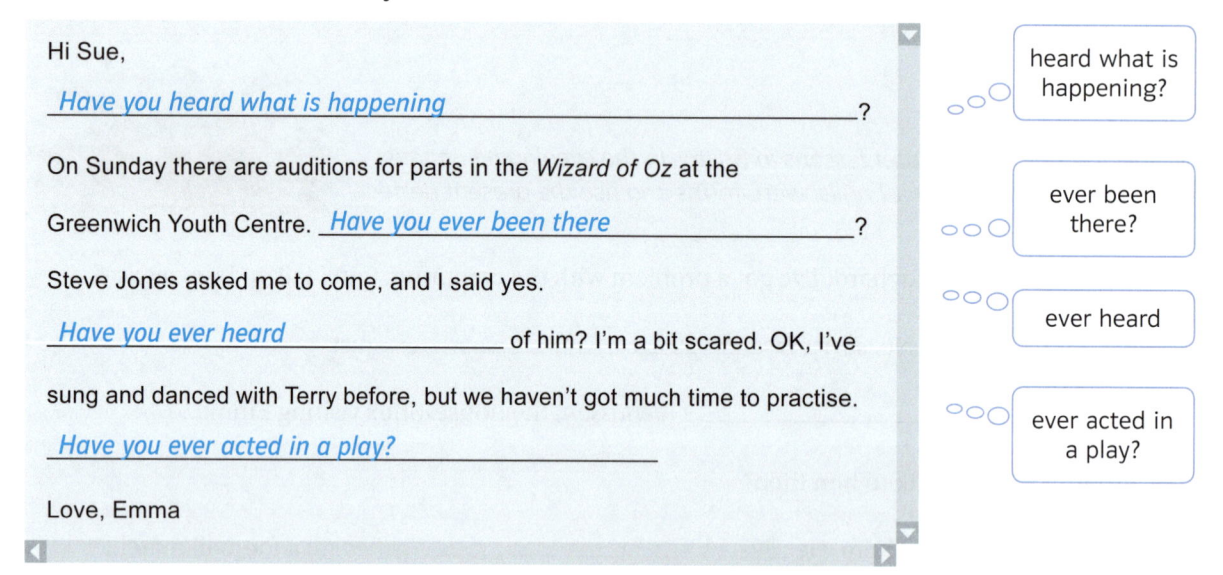

Hi Sue,

__Have you heard what is happening__ ?   [heard what is happening?]

On Sunday there are auditions for parts in the *Wizard of Oz* at the Greenwich Youth Centre. __Have you ever been there__ ?   [ever been there?]

Steve Jones asked me to come, and I said yes. __Have you ever heard__ of him? I'm a bit scared. OK, I've sung and danced with Terry before, but we haven't got much time to practise. __Have you ever acted in a play?__   [ever heard] [ever acted in a play?]

Love, Emma

12 Terry wants to know (→ p. 67/ex. 3)

Terry is asking Nasreen a lot of questions. What does he say?

1. Emma • ever • the • been • has • to Greenwich Youth Centre?
2. Emma • has • already • come back • from Bristol?
3. already • Emma • found • her • has • mobile?
4. English homework • done • Emma • has • already • her?

1. __Has Emma ever been to the Greenwich Youth Centre?__
2. __Has Emma already come back from Bristol?__
3. __Has Emma already found her mobile?__
4. __Has Emma already done her English homework?__

13 A survey (→ p. 67/ex. 3)

a) *Answer the following questions about yourself¹.* **(Lösungsvorschlag)**

Example: Have you ever been to Bristol? – Yes, I have. • No, I haven't.

1. Have you ever watched a film in English? _Yes, I have._
2. Have you ever visited London? _No, I haven't._
3. Have you ever downloaded songs from the Internet? _Yes, I have._
4. Have you ever lost your mobile? _No, I haven't._
5. Have you ever eaten fish and chips? _No, I haven't._
6. Have you ever taken pictures with a digital camera? _Yes, I have._

b) *Work in groups and ask your partners these questions. Fill in 'yes' or 'no'.* **(Lösungsvorschlag)**

name / question	Tom	Tina	Lisa	Sue
1.	yes	no	yes	no
2.	yes	yes	no	no
3.	no	yes	yes	yes
4.	no	no	no	yes
5.	yes	no	yes	no
6.	no	yes	no	no

c) *Write a text about your friends' answers.* **(Lösungsvorschlag)**

Example: Anna has already watched a film in English.
Jens and Paul haven't watched a film in English/have never watched a film in English.

Tom has already watched a film in English. Tom and Tina have already visited London but Tom has never downloaded songs from the Internet. Lisa has never lost her mobile phone. Tom has already eaten fish and chips but has never taken pictures with a digital camera.

¹yourself [jɔːˈself] – *dich selbst*

5 | Check-in | **Language** | Story | Wordwise | Check-out

14 Let's listen: Don't worry! (→ p. 67/ex. 4) (HV-Text S. 87)

a) *Listen to the text. Who wants to know these things?*

1. Has Nasreen closed all the windows? _Mrs Brook_
2. Has Rob switched off all the computers in the shop? _Mrs Brook_
3. Has Nasreen seen Emma's mobile? _Emma_
4. Has Mr Richards phoned? _Mr Brook_
5. Has Mrs Brook seen Nasreen's camera? _Nasreen_
6. Has Emma borrowed Nasreen's camera? _Mrs Brook_

b) *Which of these pictures are correct? Make a ✓ next to the correct picture.*

1. Nasreen has closed every … .   (✓ window)
3. Mr Richards wanted to pick up his … .   (✓ laptop)
2. Richard has switched off every … in the shop.   (✓ computer)
4. Nasreen is looking for her … .   (✓ camera)

15 So many questions! (→ p. 68/ex. 3)

*The Taylors have gone away and only Barker is at home. He has done some crazy things.
Look at the picture and the words in the box. Make questions and use the present perfect.*

1. Where • he • put • the shoe?
2. What • he • eat?
3. Where • he • leave • his ball?
4. What • he • do • with the magazine?
5. Who • he • invite?

1. _Where has he put the shoe?_
2. _What has he eaten?_
3. _Where has he left his ball?_
4. _What has he done with the magazine?_
5. _Who has he invited?_

16 Let's talk: An Interview (→ p. 68/ex. 3)

Ask each other questions and let your partner give the answers.
You can find the information in the pictures or in the key words. Partner A starts.

A

you • ever • be • to a play?

(Yes, I have. Have you ever acted in a play?)

you • go • to an audition?

(Yes, I have. Have you ever used a wig?)

record • your voice?

(No, I haven't. Have you ever watched *The Wizard of Oz*?)

you • see • all the *Star Wars* films?

(Yes, I have. Have you seen all the *James Bond* films?)

you • be • in a TV studio?

(Yes, I have.)

B

(Have you ever been to a play?)

act • in a play?

(No, I haven't. Have you ever gone to an audition?)

you • use • a wig?

(Yes, I have. Have you ever recorded your voice?)

you • watch • *The Wizard of Oz*?

(No, I haven't. Have you seen all the *Star Wars* films?)

you • see • all the *James Bond* films?

(No, I haven't. Have you ever been in a TV studio?)

(Have you ever been in a TV studio?)

A

Where • put … ?

(I've put it in my school bag. What have you done to your hair?)

I • … • it.

What • bought … ?

(I've bought some milk. Who has eaten the sausages?)

… • eat them.

B

(Where have you put my MP3 player?)

I • put • in … .

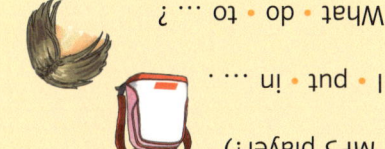

What • do • to … ?

(I've dyed it. What have you bought?)

I • buy • … .

Who • eat … ?

(The dog has eaten them.)

17 Terry's dream (→ p. 71/ex. 3)

a) *Read the text.*

Terry is dog-tired after the audition. It has been a long day. After supper he plays his favourite computer game and goes to bed early. He soon has an interesting dream … .

Terry has gone to Hollywood for an audition with Jake Martin, a famous director[1]. Everything in Hollywood is big and strange. Terry is nervous. He wants to have a part in the next Spiderman film. He is waiting for his audition in the studio when a man comes past.

"Hi," he says. "Are you waiting for someone?"
"Yes, I've got an audition at 2 o'clock for a part in the new Spiderman film."
"Oh, but it's only 12 o'clock. Are you English?"
"Yes, my name's Terry. I'm from Greenwich."
"Oh, I lived in London once. Let's go to the cafeteria and have a burger and a coke, and you can tell me how London has changed. The auditions start at 2 o'clock, so you've got a lot of time."
"OK. I feel a bit hungry. A burger and coke – that's a brilliant idea."
Terry tells him all about Greenwich. The man is very interested and asks a lot of questions.
Then he says, "Oh, it's half past one. It's time to go back to work. See you!"

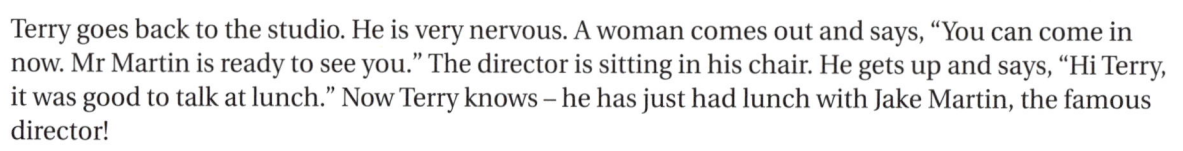

Terry goes back to the studio. He is very nervous. A woman comes out and says, "You can come in now. Mr Martin is ready to see you." The director is sitting in his chair. He gets up and says, "Hi Terry, it was good to talk at lunch." Now Terry knows – he has just had lunch with Jake Martin, the famous director!

And then Terry wakes up … .

b) *Answer the questions.*

1. How does Terry feel after the audition? _Terry is dog-tired._

2. How does he feel before the audition in Hollywood? _He is nervous._

3. Why does Terry go to the cafeteria with the man? _He feels hungry._

4. Who is the man? _He is a famous director._

18 SKILLS: Make notes (→ p. 71/ex. 4)

Make notes on the audition for the new Spiderman film.

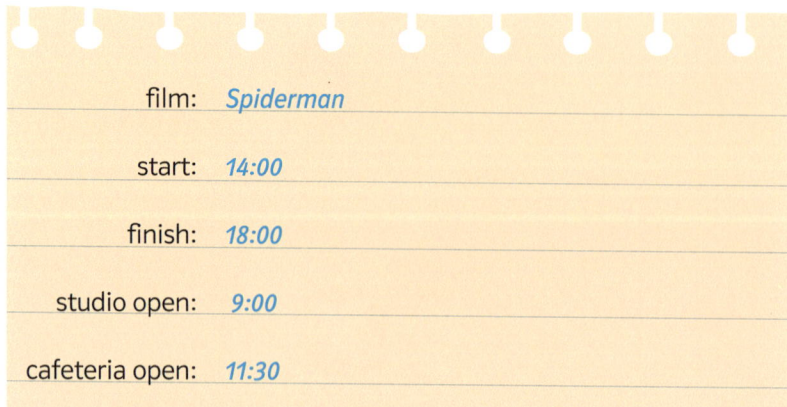

film:	Spiderman
start:	14:00
finish:	18:00
studio open:	9:00
cafeteria open:	11:30

The audition for SPIDER-MAN starts at 14:00 and finishes at 18:00.
The studio opens at 9:00.
Our cafeteria opens at 11:30.
Good luck !

[1] director [dɪˈrektə] – *Regisseur*

19 SKILLS: Which verb? (→ p. 72/ex. 1)

Choose the right verb: 'do', 'make' or 'take'. Use the third form.

1. Have you _done_ your homework yet?
2. Sorry, I think I've _made_ a mistake.
3. They have _done_ a lot of sports and now they are tired.
4. What have you _done_ with my MP3 player?
5. I've just _taken_ a photo of Grandma.
6. I've already _made_ a list. It can help you buy the things for the weekend.

20 Opposites (→ p. 72/ex. 2)

Give the opposites of the following words.

1. to push ↔ _to pull_
2. to drop ↔ _to pick up_
3. to bring ↔ _to take away_
4. to close ↔ _to open_
5. to love ↔ _to hate_
6. cheap ↔ _expensive_
7. easy ↔ _difficult_
8. hot ↔ _cold_
9. interesting ↔ _boring_
10. long ↔ _short_

21 Secret[1] text messages (→ p. 72/ex. 3)

Terry and Sam are sending secret messages to each other. What do they mean?

```
1. R U OK?
2. I cn C U 2.
3. R U cmng 4 T 2-day?
4. I 8 bscts 4 T.
5. R U X-cited?
6. U cn B a DJ!
```

1. _Are you OK?_
2. _I can see you too._
3. _Are you coming for tea today?_
4. _I ate biscuits for tea._
5. _Are you excited?_
6. _You can be a DJ!_

[1] secret ['si:krət] – geheim

5 Check-out

22 Tom's day (→ p. 73/ex. 1)

Look at the pictures and say what Tom has or hasn't done.

1. `pick` — *Tom has picked some flowers.*
2. `wash` — *Tom hasn't washed the car.*
3. `paint` — *Tom has painted the walls.*
4. `clean` — *Tom hasn't cleaned his room.*
5. `eat`   — *Tom has eaten some chocolate.*
6. `feed` — *Tom hasn't fed Barker.*

23 Have you done it? (→ p. 73/ex. 3)

When Lisa's mum comes home, she asks Lisa some questions. What are her questions? What does Lisa answer?

Have you done your homework?

Yes, I have. (do your homework 🙂)

Have you done the shopping?

No, I haven't. (do the shopping ☹)

Have you played with Jade?

Yes, I have. (play with Jade 🙂)

Have you cleaned the kitchen?

Yes, I have. (clean the kitchen 🙂)

Have you washed the clothes?

No, I haven't. (wash the clothes ☹)

Unit 6 It's our world!

1 Emma's mail (→ p. 74/text)

Read Emma's mail to Fiona and fill in the missing words.

Word box: flash, floods, ponies, trip, power, moors, wet, environment, miles, blanket, rubber, boots

Hi Fiona,

Now it's only a week before our trip to Exmoor and the boys are going bananas! Terry is a real __wet__ __blanket__. He's mad because Exmoor is __miles__ from the nearest town. He wants to stay here. But we've already learned a lot about the weather, __flash__ __floods__ and water __power__ here in Greenwich, so what? I think Terry is panicking because Tracy Brown isn't coming on the __trip__. Sam's biggest problem is that he hasn't got any __rubber__ __boots__. He knows that the __environment__ is important and he likes walking. But I think that he's scared. He doesn't like walking on the __moors__. Lisa and I want to ride __ponies__ there every day. That'll be good fun!

Love, Emma

2 A class trip (→ p. 75/ex. 4)

Write about a class trip. Read the text and fill in the missing words. You can use the words from the grid or choose your own words. (Lösungsvorschlag)

__Last week__ we went on a class trip to __Hamburg__. We stayed there __for 3 days__. The weather was __fine__. Our trip was __nice__. We __visited a church__. It was really __boring__ there. My friend and I __played tricks__ and later we __watched a film__. It was a really __great__ trip!

Where?	What?	How?	When?	How long?
– Berlin • Hamburg – the zoo • the museum – an ice hockey match	– visit some interesting places • a church – have fun – go swimming – play games – watch a film – play tricks	– nice • good • great – fine – warm • cold – terrible • boring – sunny • rainy – fantastic	– in spring • summer • autumn • winter – last week • month • year – on Monday • Tuesday • … – in January • February • …	– for … day(s) • weeks • months • a weekend

3 In the street (→ p. 76/ex. 1)

Look at the picture. What will or won't happen?
Use the words in the boxes and make sentences with 'will' and 'won't'.

1. Terry _will miss_ the bus.
2. Emma _will drop_ the sweets.
3. Barker _will get_ a sausage.
4. Lisa _will eat_ the chips.
5. Tiger _won't catch_ Tom.
6. It _won't rain_.
7. Sam _won't meet_ Emma.
8. Emma _won't see_ the car.

| won't catch |
| will get |
| will drop |
| will miss |
| won't see |
| won't rain |
| won't meet |
| will eat |

4 A tongue twister (→ p. 76/ex. 1)

Try to say this tongue twister.

On a wet windy Wednesday in West Wiltshire Will will watch wicked wizards who won't work without wigs.

5 Breakfast at the centre (→ p. 77/ex. 3)

Who promises to help with the breakfast? Fill in the verbs and 'I'll' or 'we'll'.

Verbs: make, put, wash, bring, clean, take

1. Emma: "_I'll bring_ the sausages, Mr Rose."
2. Sam and Terry: "_We'll put_ the bread on the table, Mr Rose."
3. Lisa: "_I'll make_ the tea, Mr Rose."
4. Emma and Sam: "_We'll wash_ the plates and the other things, Mr Rose."
5. Terry and Lisa: "_We'll take_ the rubbish outside, Mr Rose."
6. Sam: "_I'll clean_ the kitchen floor, Mr Rose."

6 That's OK, Mr Rose! (→ p. 77/ex. 4)

What do they answer Mr Rose? Complete the sentences with 'won't' and the right verb.

1. "Emma, don't forget the sausages, please."

   "That's OK, Mr Rose. I _won't forget_ them."

2. "Peter and Martin, look at the plates. They'll break."

   "Don't worry, Mr Rose. We _won't break_ them."

3. "Lisa, watch the hot water. You'll hurt your fingers."

   "No problem, Mr Rose. I _won't hurt_ them."

4. "Peter, please don't lose any more rubbish on your way outside."

   "I'm sorry, Mr Rose. I _won't lose_ anything more now."

5. "Martin, don't forget to clean the floor under the table, please."

   "That's OK, Mr Rose. I _won't forget_ it."

7 Opposites (→ p. 77/ex. 4)

Peter always thinks that good things will happen. Martin is always sure that bad things will happen. Look at the sentences. What will Peter and Martin say? Use 'I'm sure' and 'I think'.

- never see them again
- forget all my words
- have fun in the school play
- be too difficult for me
- have to walk in the rain
- know the right answers
- get home before it rains ✓
- find their way home

1. They are out in the park and there are dark clouds.

   Peter: _I think I'll get home before it rains._

   Martin: _I'm sure I'll have to walk in the rain._

2. There is a Maths test tomorrow.

   Peter: _I think I'll know the right answers._

   Martin: _I'm sure it'll be too difficult for me._

3. They can't find their dogs in the park.

   Peter: _I think they'll find their way home._

   Martin: _I'm sure I'll never see them again._

4. They have got parts in the school play.

   Peter: _I think I'll have fun in the school play._

   Martin: _I'm sure I'll forget all my words._

8 What will the weather be like on Friday? (→ p. 78/text)

Read the forecast in your book on page 78. Then put a ✓ next to the right symbols.

	rain clouds	rain/overcast	temperature	sun/clear
early morning		✓	✓ (8°-10°C)	
later	clouds	✓ (sun)	rain clouds	✓ (15°-18°C)
early evening	✓ (rain)	✓ (clouds)		✓ (wind/cloud)
by midnight	sun	15°-18°C	✓ (rain)	overcast

9 A puzzle (→ p. 78/text)

Fill in the correct words.

Across (→)
1. When there is a lot of wind it is … .
3. When the police do not catch a person, he can … .
5. … is twelve o'clock at night.
7. When it is cold outside, you need … in your rooms.
9. When the weatherman says what the weather will be like the following days he/she makes a … .
11. When you talk about the temperature you use … Celsius.
13. The opposite of 'fall' is … .

Down (↓)
2. When you use 'degree Celsius' you talk about the … .
4. In autumn there is often … .
6. You do it with your arms, hands, fingers, legs, feet … .
8. The opposite of 'near' is … .
10. When it rains it usually is …, too.
12. When there is a lot of … coming down it is wet outside.

1. STORMY
3. ESCAPE
5. MIDNIGHT
7. HEATING
9. FORECAST
11. DEGREE
13. RISE

10 Let's listen: Three days later (→ p. 78/ex. 1) (HV-Text S. 87)

a) *What text did you hear?*

a radio play ☐   the news ☐   a weather forecast ✔

b) *Listen and find out what the weather will be like tomorrow. Put a ✔ next to the right symbols.*

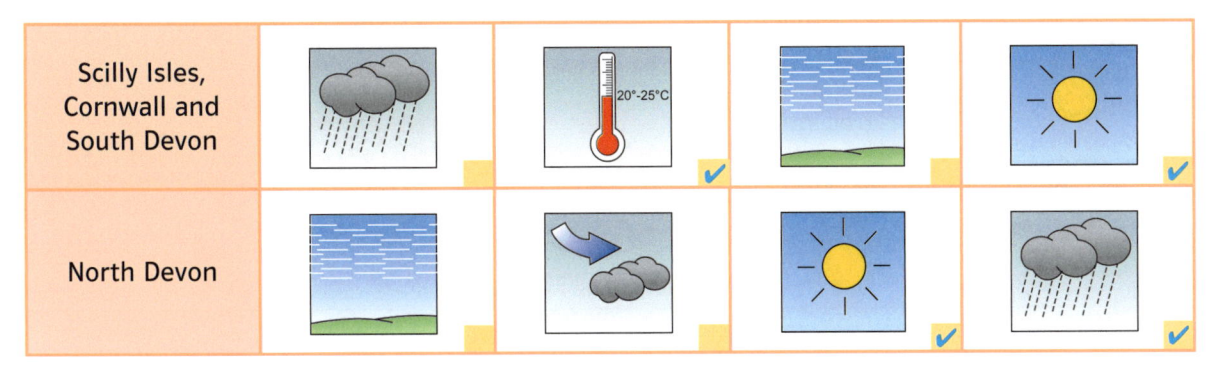

Scilly Isles, Cornwall and South Devon		✔		✔
North Devon				✔	✔

c) *Write a weather forecast in your exercise book. Use the following words.* (Lösungsvorschlag S. 86)

tomorrow — in the morning — in the afternoon — sunny — 20–25°C — will — rainy — warm — temperature

sixty-seven 67

6 Language

11 Mr Rose, will …? (→ p. 78/ex. 2)

The children have got a lot of questions. Write them down and complete Mr Rose's answers. Work with a partner.

1. trip • be very long? — Mr Rose, will our trip be very long? • No, it won't.
2. it • be wet on the paths? — Will it be wet on the paths ? • Yes, it will.
3. we • need rubber boots? — Will we need rubber boots ? • Yes, you will.
4. the farm • be interesting? — Will the farm be interesting ? • Yes, it will.
5. we • see ponies there? — Will we see ponies there ? • No, you won't.
6. there • be toilets there? — Will there be toilets there ? • Yes, there will.
7. we • come home late? — Will we come home late ? • No, we won't.

12 Late again! (→ p. 78/ex. 3)

Sam and Terry didn't hear what Mr Rose said. What are their questions?

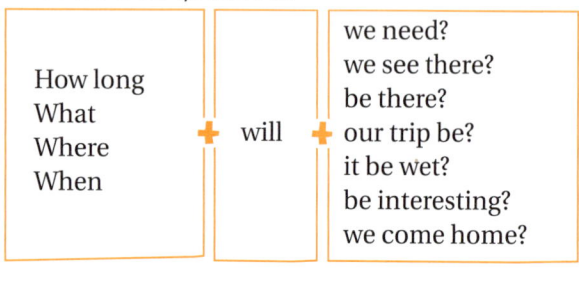

| How long / What / Where / When | + will + | we need? / we see there? / be there? / our trip be? / it be wet? / be interesting? / we come home? |

1. What will we need?
2. What will we see there?
3. When will we be there?
4. How long will our trip be?
5. Where will it be wet?
6. What will be interesting?
7. When will we come home?

13 Questions for you (→ p. 78/ex. 3)

a) *Read the questions and write down the answers.*   *(Lösungsvorschlag)*

1. How old will you be on your next birthday? _12_
2. When will the next birthday in your family be? _16th June_
3. When (what month) will the next Friday the 13th be? _July_
4. Where will you be at nine o'clock tomorrow morning? _at school_
5. When will you have your next Art lesson? _tomorrow_
6. Where will you be on December 25th this year? _at home_

b) *Compare your answers with your partner's answers. Which answers are the same? Which answers are different?* *(individuelle Schülerlösung)*

14 A horoscope for you (→ p. 80/ex. 1)

will be   will play   will test   will be

Here is your horoscope for the next week. Read what it says and fill in the correct verbs.

Your teacher _will be_ very nice this week but don't forget your homework on Wednesday because your teacher _will test_ you. Be careful! Someone _will play_ a trick on you on Friday but the weekend _will be_ fantastic.

15 What can you say? (→ p. 80/ex. 1)

Match the sentences with the pictures and compare your answers with your partner's answers.

Be careful!   Stay calm.   Don't worry!   Use your head.

Be careful!    _Use your head._

Don't worry!    _Stay calm._

6 | Check-in | **Language** | Story | Wordwise | Check-out

16 Phoning the Exmoor Weather Line[1] (→ p. 81/ex. 1)

Work with a partner. Partner A is the weatherman, partner B is a tourist. The tourist phones the Exmoor Weather Line for information on the weather. Say the German sentences in English. Your partner checks your English sentences. Partner A starts.

A – Weatherman

Melde dich am Telefon mit „Exmoor Weather Line" und nenne deinen Namen.

(Hello, my name is … .)

Frage, was du für ihn/sie tun kannst.

(I want to go on a bike trip tomorrow. What will the weather be like?)

Sage, dass es morgens regnen wird.

(There is always rain on Exmoor.)

Sage, dass es nachmittags sonnig sein wird.

(That's great. Thank you very much. Bye!)

Verabschiede dich.

B – Tourist

(Hello, Exmoor Weather Line. This is … .)

Sage hallo und nenne deinen Namen.

(What can I do for you?)

Sage, dass du morgen eine Radtour machen willst und frage nach den Wetteraussichten.

(It'll be rainy in the morning.)

Sage, dass es in Exmoor immer regnet.

(It'll be sunny in the afternoon.)

Sage, dass du dich freust und bedanke dich. Verabschiede dich.

(Bye!)

[1] weather line [ˈweðə ˌlaɪn] – *Wetterdienst*

| Check-in | Language | **Story** | Wordwise | Check-out | **6** |

17 Emma's dream (→ p. 82/before the text)

Emma has a dream. She's in a very old dark house and there's an old woman with a crystal ball[1]. She's telling her the future.

a) Before you read the text "The rescue" in your book, do this exercise.
   What does the old woman tell Emma?

> Crystal ball, crystal ball, show us here and now!
> What is in the future, where and who and how?
> Good luck or bad luck? – What will our luck be?
> Crystal ball, show me so that we can see.
> Crystal ball, Emma is here and wants to know,
> What future days will bring her,
> and where her paths will go.

> Let me see. Oh, yes! You'll go on a trip, Emma. It won't be a long trip. I see water, a lot of water. You won't be very happy. There will be some people with you. Water will play an important role. I'm sorry to say that you'll all have a problem. But you will have a great idea and everything will be OK in the end.

b) Do you want to know what the old woman is talking about?
   Read the text "The rescue" and find out.

18 The old woman's advice (→ p. 83/text)

Do you know now what the old woman is talking about? Write it down.

The old woman talked about:	What happened in the story:
the trip:	Emma is on a class trip with her friends.
a lot of water:	It's raining. Emma and her friends are on a small island in the river.
some people:	Terry, Emma, Sam and Lisa are in a group with Peter and Martin.
A problem:	There is a flash flood and they are trapped on an island.
Emma's great idea:	She waves her pink umbrella.
OK in the end:	A helicopter rescues them.

19 My storybook: On an island in the north (→ p. 83/ex. 3)

You are going to an island in the north and you must carry your things in your bag. You can only take 10 things. What will you take with you? Say why. Write in your exercise book. *(individuelle Schülerlösung)*

---

[1] crystal ball [ˌkrɪstəl ˈbɔːl] – *Kristallkugel*

6 | Check-in | Language | Story | Wordwise | Check-out

20 Double puzzle (→ p. 84/ex. 2)

a) *Do the weather puzzle.*

NAYRI	R₆	A₇	I₁₁	N	Y
NYNSU	S	U	N	N	Y
GYFGO	F	O	G	G	Y
NYDWI	W₁	I	N	D	Y
CUDLOY	C	L	O	U	D₈	Y
TYRMOS	S	T₄	O	R	M	Y

SOYNW	S₁₂	N	O	W	Y
TOH	H₅	O	T
CLDO	C₉	O	L	D
RMWA	W	A₃	R	M
WTE	W	E₂	T₁₀

b) *Fill in the correct letters.*

| W₁ | E₂ | A₃ | T₄ | H₅ | E₂ | R₆ |

| A₇ | D₈ | J | E₂ | C₉ | T₁₀ | I₁₁ | V | E₂ | S₁₂ |

21 Guessing game (→ p. 84/ex. 3)

Work with a partner.

a) *Read the sentences to your partner. Your partner writes down the correct word.*

1. It's everywhere around us outside.   e n v i r o n m e n t
2. It's land with water all around it.   i s l a n d
3. When you leave it you're nice and fresh.   s h o w e r
4. The south of Germany often gets a lot of it in the winter.   s n o w
5. It's very important to most girls.   f a s h i o n
6. A short text which tells you what will happen.   h o r o s c o p e
7. You need it when it rains.   u m b r e l l a

b) *Now your partner makes sentences and you guess the correct word.*

1. rooms • warm — It makes rooms warm. — heating
2. small river — It's a small river. — stream
3. 1.609 km — It's 1.609 km. — mile
4. hard • heavy — It's hard and heavy. — stone
5. little horse — It's a little horse. — pony
6. girls • like — Girls like it. — fashion
7. girls • use — Girls use it. — lip balm

22 A 1st May party (→ p. 85/ex. 1)

*Lisa and Emma are planning a garden party for 1st May.
Read the text and fill in 'will' or 'won't'.*

Lisa: What do you think? How many people __will__ come?

Emma: I think there __will__ be nine. You and me, Linda and Molly and the five boys.

Lisa: Linda and Molly __won't__ eat a lot, but I'm sure the boys __will__ be hungry.

Emma: I've got an idea. Let's ask the others to help. I'm sure they __will__ all bring some food.

Lisa: Great! That __will__ save money and we __won't__ have to carry all the heavy plates outside into the garden. What do you think the others __will__ say about our idea?

Emma: I'm sure they __will__ like it. Sam __will__ be happy. He can make a chocolate cake.

Lisa: OK then. I __will__ talk to the girls and you can talk to the boys.

23 Promises, promises (→ p. 85/ex. 1)

William the wolf[1] likes Sheila[2] the sheep. What does he ask her? And what does Sheila answer?

- show me your shed
- go to the moors with me
- tell the other sheep about me
- meet me tonight
- run away

1. __Will you show me your shed__? No, I won't.
2. __Will you go to the moors with me?__ No, I won't.
3. __Will you meet me tonight?__ No, I won't.
4. __Will you tell the other sheep about me?__ Yes, I will.
5. __Will you run away?__ Yes, I will.

[1] wolf [wʊlf] – *Wolf*; [2] Sheila [ʃiːlə] – *weiblicher Vorname*

Revision 3

1 Third forms (→ p. 86/ex. 1)

The letters of the verbs are not in the right order. Can you correct them?

| break | go | make | wash | send | finish |

1. My T-shirt is dirty! Mum hasn't sedwah it yet. _washed_
2. Have you already nedfishi your homework? _finished_
3. I'm very sorry. I've just nekorb a glass. _broken_
4. Have you already nest the letter to Berlin? _sent_
5. Lisa is still in her room. She hasn't noge to her friends yet. _gone_
6. Oh, we've just dame a mistake! _made_

2 Whose place is it? (→ p. 86/ex. 3)

a) *Look at the three rooms. Then read the text and find out which boy lives in which room. Write the correct names under the pictures.*

1. _Paul_

2. _Nick_

3. _Jack_

| Jack | Nick | Paul |

Nick has closed his window. Jack has made his bed. Paul has put his books in his bag. Nick has made his bed. Jack and Paul haven't cleaned their desks but their books are in their school bags. Nick has already cleaned his desk but he hasn't put his books in his bag. Jack hasn't closed the window but Paul has.

b) *What will the boys do next? Write the sentences in your exercise book.*
   Start like this: Jack will clean his desk …   (Lösungsvorschlag S. 86)

| Check-in | Language | Story | Wordwise | Check-out | **7** |

Unit 7   A holiday in Ireland

1 Two families (→ p. 88/text)

Underline the wrong information in the sentences and write down the correct information.

1. The O'Briens' <u>grandad</u> made a play room in the barn.   <u>Mr O'Brien</u>

2. <u>Mr Lehmann</u> comes from Dublin.   <u>Mrs Lehmann</u>

3. The <u>O'Briens</u> have got ponies.   <u>The farmer</u>

4. The Lehmanns want to visit <u>Northern Ireland</u>.   <u>the west coast of Ireland</u>

5. The O'Briens sometimes go swimming in a <u>lake</u>.   <u>the sea</u>

2 Two dialogues (→ p. 89/ex. 2)

a) *Two dialogues are mixed here. Find the sentences for each dialogue and put them in the correct order.*

- **2** That's a good idea. But why?
- **4** Yes, and you like to play team sports. I'd rather go swimming.
- **2** Why? I'd rather be in a big city.
- **1** I'd like to learn how to play cricket.
- **1** I'd like to go camping in my summer holidays.
- **3** Because I like to learn new things and it's more exciting than football.
- **4** That's a good idea, but I'd like to have some exciting things around me in the holidays.
- **3** Because I want to have some peace and quiet.

b) *Practise the dialogues with a partner.*

3 Let's listen: What's wrong? (→ p. 89/ex. 3)

Match the pictures with the texts. There are two more texts than pictures.

1. But finish your lunch first.
2. I'll turn on the computer.
3. Limerick is miles from Dublin. It's probably a dump.
4. Christoph, you haven't eaten your lunch. Are you feeling sick?
5. Oh! Don't be a wet blanket!
6. We'll go to Dublin.

A	B	C	D
4	3	2	1

7 Language

4 Making adverbs (→ p. 90/ex. 1)

Make adverbs from these words.

happy	happily	quick	quickly
busy	busily	clear	clearly
quiet	quietly	angry	angrily
worried	worriedly	bad	badly
helpful	helpfully	beautiful	beautifully
hungry	hungrily	cheap	cheaply
nervous	nervously	correct	correctly
careful	carefully	excited	excitedly

5 Barny, the ghost in the O'Briens' barn (→ p. 91/ex. 2)

This is a day in the life of the ghost. Make adverbs and complete the activities.
The adjectives in the ghost will help you. There are more adjectives than you will need.

5:00 – 18:00 sleep under the roof _quietly_
18:00 get up _quickly_
19:00 have breakfast _hungrily_
21:00 sing new ghost songs _beautifully_
23:00 watch the people _carefully_
midnight shout _loudly_
1:00 frighten the people _terribly_
2:00 whisper _softly_
4:00 fly around _busily_
5:00 go to bed _tiredly_

(Adjectives in the ghost: careful, tired, busy, loud, healthy, clear, terrible, quiet, beautiful, quick, hungry, soft)

Check-in | **Language** | Story | Wordwise | Check-out

6 Weather rules (→ p. 91/ex. 3)

Put the rhyming pairs together and write them in your exercise book. Write down what it means in German. Underline the verbs in your sentences and tell your partner what tense it is. (Lösung S. 86)

If it starts out foggy grey¹,	it will rain for thirty days together.	If the morning is grey and the evening red,
it will stop by eleven.	If it rains before seven,	it will be a good weather day.
If St. Vitus's Day² is rainy weather,	in winter there will be a storm.	If a cold August follows a hot July,
there will be a winter hard and dry³.	If the first week in August is very warm,	the weather won't make you stay in bed.

7 What are Christoph and Helen saying? (→ p. 91/ex. 3)

a) *Put in the correct verb forms. The colours can help you.*

is | stay | wants | aren't | will tell | will go | will stay | will phone

1. If we only _stay_ in Limerick, I _will go_ bananas.
2. If Mum _wants_ to go to a castle every day, I _will stay_ at the house.
3. If Hannah _is_ a pain, I _will tell_ Mum and Dad.
4. If there _aren't_ any kids, I _will phone_ my friends at home every day.

b) *Helen is making a plan for the Lehmanns' holidays. What does she think?*

1. If the Lehmanns _go_ to the farm, they _will see_ the ponies. (go • see)
2. If they _hear_ strange noises, they _will think_ it is a ghost. (hear • think)
3. If they _are_ bored, they _will love_ our play room. (be • love)
4. If the weather _is_ hot, they _will go_ to the sea. (be • go)

8 Let's listen: Ready for Limerick (→ p. 91/ex. 4)

Which sentences are right and which are wrong?

1. Mrs Lehmann wants to spend time in Limerick. — **R** W
2. Christoph is not excited about Limerick. — **R** W
3. The children near the farmhouse are friendly. — **R** W
4. Mr Lehmann isn't happy about all the lakes⁴. — R **W**
5. Christoph thinks the lakes will be fantastic. — R **W**
6. Christoph wants to meet the girl at the street fair. — R **W**

¹grey [greɪ] – *grau*; ²St. Vitus's Day [snt ˈvaɪtəsɪz ˌdeɪ] – 15ᵗʰ *June*; ³dry [draɪ] – *trocken*; ⁴lake [leɪk] – *See*

7 | Check-in | **Language** | Story | Wordwise | Check-out

9 Let's talk: A quiz (→ p. 92/ex. 1)

Work with a partner. Read the questions to your partner and check his/her answers. Give your partner one point for each correct answer. The partner who gets the most points wins.

> The answers are all somewhere in your book or in your workbook.

A

1. Who wore a blond wig in *The Lord of the Rings*?
   Orlando Bloom

2. You know this sheep from one of your exercises. What's her name?
   Sheila

3. What is the capital city of Ireland?
   Dublin

4. Who feels sick in Unit 3?
   a kangaroo

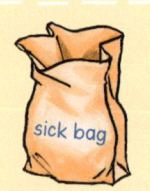

5. What's this?
   a leprechaun

6. Which food does Sam hate?
   fish

7. What is 'Aquarius' in German?
   Wassermann

8. In Unit 3 of your workbook there is a recipe for … .
   pizza

B

1. You know this wolf from one of your exercises. What is his name?
   William

2. What is Jake's family name?
   Howard

3. What is the capital city of Germany?
   Berlin

4. Who was Elizabeth I?
   Queen of England

5. Where is the Flight Lab?
   Science Museum in London

6. What is the name of the TV soap with Phoebe, Monica, Rachel, Ross, Joey and Chandler?
   Friends

7. Who plays the lion in *The Wizard of Oz*?
   Terry

8. What is the name of the ghost in the O'Briens' barn?
   Barry

10 SKILLS: Information from pictures (→ p. 92/ex. 1)

Look at the pictures and think about the questions. Write notes under the pictures.
Then describe one of the pictures in your exercise book.   *(Lösungsvorschlag)*

1. What can you see in the picture?
2. What is happening in the picture?
3. Where do you think the people/the animals are?
4. How do they feel?
5. What do you think they are saying/thinking?
6. What happened before and what will happen later?

A

There are three boys. Two boys are angry. The boy with the brown jacket wants to hit the boy on the left. The boy in the middle is strapping him. I think they will be friends again.

B

There are four girls in a shop. They are looking at trousers. The girls are happy. They are talking about the size of the trousers. I think they will put on some trousers next.

C

There are two boys and one girl. They are playing football. The girl and one boy are in the same team. They are happy. Next the girl will kick the ball.

D

There is a cat and a dog. They are sleeping together. They are having a nice dream. Next they will wake up.

11 Limericks for lunch (→ p. 95/ex. 3)

Read the text.

Mr and Mrs Chapman and their three children, Tim, Thomas and Tess were not happy. They were lost somewhere in Ireland on a little country road. They wanted to go to Bruff but they just couldn't find the right way. Suddenly Mrs Chapman shouted, "Daniel, be careful! What is that man doing?"

Mr Chapman stopped the car and they all looked at the strange man. He waved his arms crazily and jumped up and down. He had a friendly smile but he looked very strange. The man started to say something but the family couldn't hear him through their car windows. Mr Chapman put his window down but Mrs Chapman stopped him.

"Daniel, the man is crazy. Put your window back up," she said nervously.
"I'll stay in the car, Mary, I just want to ask him the way to Bruff," Mr Chapman answered. As soon as the window was down, they could hear the man. He said:

"Now you can hear me clearly.
And I can see you nearly¹.
Why not come out
Then I must not shout
The introductions: I'm O'Leary!"

The children laughed loudly and quickly jumped out of the car before Mrs Chapman could stop them. "I'm Tim, this is Thomas and our little sister Tess," Tim, the oldest of the Chapman children, said excitedly. Mr and Mrs Chapman got out of the car, too. Mr Chapman asked Mr O'Leary for the way to Bruff.

This was Mr O'Leary's answer:
"Here you are in Rathkeale
On the road to Abbeyfeale.
But to get out to Bruff
Is really very tough².
Why not stay here for a meal?"

This time all of the Chapmans laughed. Maybe the man wasn't crazy. They left the car there and followed Mr O'Leary to his house. It was a big old house in the middle of green fields with a few trees here and there and chairs and tables in the garden. Was it a restaurant? But they were the only people there.

In another limerick Mr O'Leary explained that it was his restaurant and that Mrs O'Leary did the cooking. Mr O'Leary stopped every car that drove past and invited them to eat there. The Chapmans sat down at a table in the garden. There were no menus, but after a few minutes Mr O'Leary brought them a fantastic Irish lunch. Then he disappeared into the little house. The Chapmans had a tasty meal and they forgot all about Bruff. The children found that limericks were really easy and answered Mr O'Leary's limericks with their own limericks.

"Where do you get all the limericks from?" little Tess asked.

"The limericks aren't under my bed," said Mr O'Leary.
"Some guess they are all in his shed," said Tim.
"But if you look closely³," continued Mr O'Leary.
"You'll see that they mostly," Mrs Chapman said.
"Come jumping right out of his head," finished Thomas.

They all laughed and the Chapmans thought that this was the best day of their holiday. Then they heard another car on the country road and Mr O'Leary jumped up excitedly. He ran back to the road to stop the car and to invite the next visitors to have limericks for lunch.

---

¹nearly ['nɪəli] – *beinahe, fast*; ²tough [tʌf] – *schwierig*; ³closely ['kləʊsli] – *hier: genau*

12 SKILLS: How to understand a text (→ p. 95/ex. 3)

Put a O around the names of people **who** are in the story.	**What** do you know about them? Find the words which tell you about the people and underline them in red.	**Where** and **when** does the story happen? Find words and phrases about time and place and underline them in green.	Put a box around **key words and phrases** which you can use to **tell the story** again.

13 Tell the story (→ p. 95/ex. 4)   (Lösungsvorschlag)

Mr and Mrs Chapman and their three children, Tim, Thomas and Tess were lost on a country road in Ireland. A strange man stopped the car. He spoke in limericks. His name was O'Leary. Mrs Chapman was nervous but the children jumped out of the car. Mr Chapman asked Mr O'Leary for the way to Bruff. Mr O'Leary said that they were in Rathkeale on the road to Abbeyfeale. He invited them to his restaurant. The Chapmans left the car and went to Mr O'Leary's restaurant. Mr O'Leary brought them a fantastic lunch. The Chapmans answered Mr O'Leary's limericks with their own limericks. The Chapmans thought this was the best day of their holidays.

14 My storybook (→ p. 95/ex. 4)   (Lösungsvorschlag)

Find all the limericks in the text and underline them in blue. Choose one limerick and write it down. Draw a nice picture about the limerick.

Now you can hear me clearly.
And I can see you nearly.
Why not come out
Then I must not shout
The introductions: I'm O'Leary.

(individuelle Schülerlösung)

15 Practise adjectives (→ p. 96/ex. 2)

| popular | nervous | boring | lucky | careful | strange |

1. All the pupils like Kate and Mike. They're _popular_.
2. Mark always plays the same computer games. He's so _boring_.
3. Ian looks five times before he goes over the street. He's very _careful_.
4. Kim is holding my hand because she feels very _nervous_.
5. I'm sure I left my bag here but it's not here. That's _strange_.
6. Tim wins every game he plays. He's good, but he's also _lucky_.

16 SKILLS: Adjectives with two forms (→ p. 96/ex. 1)

Write the German meaning under the adjectives and fill in the right form in the sentences.

bored _gelangweilt_	boring _langweilig_	This book is so _boring_. I won't read it. I'm really _bored_.
excited _aufgeregt_	exciting _aufregend_	This is a very _exciting_ film. I must see it. Let's go to the cinema. I'm really _excited_.
interested _interessiert_	interesting _interessant_	Are you _interested_ in ice-hockey? – Oh yes. The London Knights' last match was very _interesting_.
surprised _überrascht_	surprising _überraschend_	What a _surprising_ present! I'm really _surprised_ that you remembered my birthday.
worried _beunruhigt_	worrying _beunruhigend_	Listen to the weather forecast. It's really _worrying_. – Oh, you needn't be _worried_. It's not for our town.

17 Signs (→ p. 97/ex. 2)

What do the signs mean? Make adverbs from the adjectives and use a verb and an adverb.

speak eat smile slow careful quiet
drive walk healthy happy

1. _drive_ _slowly_
2. _speak_ _quietly_
3. _eat_ _healthily_
4. _walk_ _carefully_
5. _smile_ _happily_

18 In Ireland (→ p. 97/ex. 2)

Complete the sentences. Fill in the right adjective or adverb.

1. Patty sings _beautifully_. She sings _beautiful_ Irish songs. (schön)
2. Dublin is a very _busy_ city. People run around _busily_. (geschäftig)
3. At the tourist information office they gave me a _quick_ answer because I needed it _quickly_. (schnell)
4. I said the Irish words _correctly_. My accent was _correct_. (richtig)
5. I think those people are _crazy_. Did you hear how they shouted _crazily_? (verrückt)
6. The sky is _clear_ today. I can see the castle _clearly_. (klar)
7. I'm very _excited_ to be in Ireland. I _excitedly_ wrote postcards to all my friends. (aufgeregt)
8. The sheep in Ireland are _quick_. They can run very _quickly_. (schnell)

Meine Lernbiografie 4

> Es ist schon erstaunlich, wie schnell so ein Schuljahr vorbei ist. Höchste Zeit, wieder die Lernbiografie fortzuführen. Du weißt ja inzwischen, wie das funktioniert.

Was ich jetzt alles kann!

Trage den entsprechenden Smiley in der entsprechenden Farbe ein.

- 🙂 **Kann ich super.**
- 😐 **Das klappt meistens.**
- ☹️ **Das ist nicht so einfach.**

		Kann ich super.	Das klappt meistens.	Das ist nicht so einfach.
Hören	Ich kann verstehen, was im Unterricht gesagt und gefragt wird.			
	Ich kann Arbeitsanweisungen meines Lehrers/meiner Lehrerin und von der CD verstehen und darauf reagieren.			
	Ich verstehe auch längere Hörtexte und kann zusammenfassen, worum es darin geht.			
	Ich kann Hörtexten auch einzelne Informationen entnehmen und Fragen zum Gehörten beantworten.			
Hören und Sehen	Ich kann Filme und Videoclips verstehen und zusammenfassen, worum es geht.			
	Ich kann Fragen zu einzelnen Informationen aus Filmen und Videoclips beantworten.			
Sprechen	Ich kann mich am Unterrichtsgespräch beteiligen.			
	Ich kann mich vorstellen, jemanden grüßen oder mich verabreden.			
	Ich kann jemanden einladen und auf Einladungen reagieren.			
	Ich kann mich an Gesprächen beteiligen, in denen es um Alltag, Schule, Freizeit und Freundschaft geht.			
	Ich kann mich in Alltagssituationen verständlich machen, z.B. bei einer Wegbeschreibung, in Restaurants, in Geschäften und in öffentlichen Verkehrsmitteln.			
	Ich kann einfache Geschichten nacherzählen.			
	Ich kann über ein wichtiges Erlebnis berichten.			
	Ich kann Personen, Gegenstände oder Ereignisse mit einfachen Sätzen beschreiben.			
	Ich kann Arbeitsergebnisse kurz und zusammenhängend präsentieren, wenn ich mich darauf vorbereitet habe.			

Lernbiografie L

Lesen	Ich kann alle Arbeitsanweisungen in meinen Englischmaterialien verstehen und entsprechend darauf reagieren.				
	Ich kann unterschiedliche Texte selbstständig lesen und das Wichtigste verstehen.				
	Ich kann auch längere Geschichten lesen und verstehen.				
	Ich kann Einzelheiten aus Texten herausfinden und Aufgaben dazu lösen.				
	Ich kann Geschichten, Gedichte und andere Texte ausdrucksvoll laut vorlesen.				
Schreiben	Ich kann einen Notizzettel schreiben, um jemanden zu informieren.				
	Ich kann Postkarten, einen einfachen persönlichen Brief oder E-Mails schreiben.				
	Ich kann einfache kürzere Texte über Erlebtes, Erlesenes oder Erfundenes für meinen *folder* schreiben.				

Und, hast du deine Lernziele aus der Lernbiografie 3 erreicht? Was war gut und was möchtest du ändern? Damit du deine guten Vorsätze nicht vergisst, schreib sie doch einfach wieder auf.

Das hat mir beim Lernen geholfen:
_____
_____

Das möchte ich weiter verbessern:
_____
_____

Tipps von meinem Lehrer / meiner Lehrerin:
_____
_____

Datum: _____ Unterschrift: _____

So, jetzt hast Du erst einmal Erholung verdient. Entspannung gehört auch zum Lernen. Also, schöne Ferien! Tschüüüüüüs!

eighty-five 85

Lösungen

Weitere Lösungen und Lösungsvorschläge:
S. 23/ex. 23 a) Last Sunday I was in the street with my friend. We found a bag with a wallet in it. In the wallet there was an address of a woman. We took the wallet to the address. The woman was very happy that she got her wallet back. **S. 29/ex. 6 b)** 1. Terry sent Jake a text message. 3. Jake had supper at Lisa's house. 5. Lisa and Jake did Jake's Maths homework. 7. Jake didn't get home before ten. **S. 34/ex. 16 b)** Picture 1 is wrong because the bullies wrote 'Scottish' accent, not 'English accent'. Picture 2 is wrong because Kate and Laura didn't send a text message. They went to the bullies and talked to them. Picture 3 is wrong because Barker was at the door of the supermarket. **S. 36/ex. 20** adoptieren, Adoption, unvergesslich, jeder, dich selbst, Spende, spenden, Abonnement, Website/Homepage, Schmetterling, Kamel, Kobra, Elefant, Giraffe, Affe, Tiger, Zebra. **S. 45/ex. 15 c)** I think they make salad and chips for lunch because they've got lettuce, tomatoes and chips. **S. 53/ex. 4 b)** to print – printed – printed, to take – took – taken, to find – found – found, to act – acted – acted, to go – went – gone. **S. 67/ex. 10 c)** Tomorrow it will be rainy in the morning. In the afternoon it will be warm and sunny and the temperature will be 20-25°C. **S. 74/ex. 2 b)** Jack will clean his desk and he will close the window. Nick will put his books in his school bag. Paul will make his bed and he will clean his desk. **S. 77/ex. 6** 1. If it starts out foggy grey, it will be a good weather day. 2. If St. Vitus's Day is rainy weather, it will rain for thirty days together. 3. If it rains before seven, it will stop by eleven. 4. If the first week in August is very warm, in winter there will be a storm. 5. If the morning is grey and the evening red, the weather won't make you stay in bed. 6. If a cold August follows a hot July, there will be a winter hard and dry.

Workbook-Hörverstehenstexte

Unit 1   S. 9/ex. 15   Let's listen: A lunch problem

At the school cafeteria

Sam: Oh no! I'm so stupid!
Emma: What's the problem, Sam?
Sam: I haven't got the money for my lunch. It's at home in my bedroom.
Emma: Oh, Sam. You always forget things.
Sam: I know. Can I borrow some money from you, please, Emma?
Emma: No, sorry. I've only got money for my lunch. But you can have some of my food.
Sam: Are you sure? Thanks, Emma. That's really nice of you. What are you having?
Emma: Let's look at the menu. What about pizza?
Sam: No, the pizzas are too small for two people.
Emma: True. And there's spaghetti. But two people can't eat spaghetti together. It's too difficult! Hm. What can we choose? Sausage and chips?
Sam: Yes, OK. Come on. – Oh, good! We're lucky.
Emma: Lucky? Why?
Sam: Mrs Green is helping in the cafeteria today. She likes me. She's always nice to me. Hello, Mrs Green.
Mrs Green: Oh hello, Sam. How are you?
Sam: Fine, thanks, Mrs Green. But – er – I'm very, very hungry today.
Mrs Green: Oh well, let's give you a nice big lunch. What do you want?
Sam: Sausage and chips, please.
Mrs Green: Here you are. Would you like another sausage?
Sam: Oh, yes, please. And chips, too. Wow! Thanks, Mrs Green. That's great. Goodbye. Come on, Emma. Now we've got lots of food!

Unit 2   S. 20/ex. 17   Let's listen: What Sam tells Lisa

Outside Thomas Tallis School

Lisa: Hi, Sam. Monday morning again! How was your weekend?
Sam: Uh.
Lisa: Hey, what's the problem, Sam? Wasn't your weekend very good?
Sam: It was OK.
Lisa: When I look at your face I'm not so sure! Where were you on Saturday?
Sam: In the park.
Lisa: And?
Sam: And Jake saw me and we had fun together with his skateboard.
Lisa: So that was good. And what about yesterday?
Sam: Yesterday afternoon Terry and I went to the cinema together.
Lisa: Well, I think you had a very nice weekend. So why are you so fed up?
Sam: I'm not fed up. I'm just – well, I had a bad night.
Lisa: A bad night? Why? Were you worried about school today?
Sam: No, I never worry about school.
Lisa: So why –
Sam: It's because yesterday evening I ate a lot of cheese. And when I eat too much cheese late in the evening I sometimes have bad dreams.
Lisa: Ah, so it was a bad dream.
Sam: Yes. It was a very long dream. I can't remember all of it. I just know it was all terrible. But I remember near the end of the dream I was in a dark corridor. And I saw an open door, so I went into the room. And there was a picture of a horrible man on the wall. And then he suddenly came out of the picture and –
Lisa: People can't come out of pictures!
Sam: They can in my dreams!
Lisa: OK, OK. Go on, Sam.
Sam: And the man was really big. And he took me and he threw me out of the window.
Lisa: And then?
Sam: I never found out. Because it was already seven o'clock this morning. And at seven o'clock Grandma always comes into my room and wakes me up. So when she came in – well, that was the end of my dream. And it was time to get up and come to school.
Lisa: There's the bell. Let's go in.
Sam: I'd rather go home and go back to my bed.
Lisa: What? And have a bad dream again?
Sam: Hm. Maybe not. Come on, then, Lisa. Tell me what we've got first this morning …

Unit 3   S. 32/ex. 13   Let's listen: Tom's day

Tom had a bad day. When he woke up, his head hurt. He went to the bathroom and washed his face. Some water got into his mouth, and it tasted terrible. When he came into the living room, he hit his elbow on the chair. Some books fell off the chair and hurt his toes. There was cheese in the kitchen, but it was old. He ate it because he was hungry. Soon his stomach hurt. Tom went outside, but it was too sunny, and so he closed his eyes. He didn't see the cat, but his ears heard a noise 'Meow!' Tom ran away, but he fell and hit his leg. He cried and jumped and hit his hands on the ground. Tom went back to the house and back to bed. It was a bad day.

Unit 4   S. 43/ex. 13   Let's listen: Five times a day

In a classroom at Thomas Tallis

Sam: You said that we should eat more fruit and vegetables. But how much should we eat?
Dr Bell: You should eat fruit and vegetables five times a day.
Sam: But that's a lot!
Dr Bell: That's right. It is a lot, Sam. That's why you must plan your day. You should start in the morning at breakfast.
Emma: I always drink a glass of juice for breakfast. Is that OK or must I eat fruit, too?
Dr Bell: Fruit juice is fine for breakfast, but the other four things shouldn't be juice.
Terry: But must it always be real juice? Lemonade has juice in it, too.
Dr Bell: It must be real juice, Terry. Lemonade is too sweet.
Lisa: But I only eat three meals a day. How can I eat fruit and vegetables five times?
Dr Bell: You needn't just eat fruit and vegetables at meals, Lisa. You can also eat them between meals.
Lisa: OK. But between meals I don't eat fruit and vegetables. I eat sweets or crisps.
Dr Bell: You shouldn't eat too many crisps and sweets, Lisa. They are not good for you. Eat an apple. That's better for you.
Terry: Well, I like apples. But I don't like other fruit and vegetables!
Dr Bell: You needn't like all fruit or vegetables, but you can't just eat apples, Terry.
Terry: I know, but …
Emma: Terry, I've got a fruit salad for lunch today. Do you want to try it?
Terry: Yes, thanks a lot, Emma.

Unit 5   S. 58/ex. 14   Let's listen: Don't worry!

Nasreen anwers the phone at home

Nasreen: Yes?
Farah: Nasreen, it's Mum here. Have you closed all the windows in the flat?
Nasreen: Yes, Mum.
Farah: And has your father switched off all the computers in the shop?
Nasreen: I'm not sure, but I can check.
Farah: Emma wants to know – have you seen her mobile?
Nasreen: No, I haven't. Has she lost it?
Farah: She's not sure. She says she can't find it in her bag or in the car.
Nasreen: OK, I can try to look for it.
Farah: Thanks. Oh, and… Just a minute. Rob is asking something.
Rob: Has Mr Richards phoned? He wanted to pick up his laptop today. I forgot about it.
Farah: Rob wants to know – has Mr Richards phoned? He wanted to pick up his laptop today.
Nasreen: No, he hasn't phoned. Mum, can I ask you something? Have you seen my digital camera? I want to take it with me to Rachel's party. I've looked in a lot of places, but I haven't found it yet. Has Emma borrowed it?
Farah: Emma, have you borrowed Nasreen's camera?
Emma: That old thing? No, I haven't.
Farah: She says, no, she hasn't. Have you looked in the cupboard in the living room? It may be there. Or look on the DVD player. I think I've seen it there.
Nasreen: OK, I can look again. Was that all?
Farah: Yes. Have fun at the party.
Nasreen: Thanks. And Mum – don't worry. Everything here is OK. Have fun in Bristol!

Unit 6   S. 67/ex. 10   Let's listen: Three days later

A weather forecaster:

Good evening. Well, I needn't tell you that it's raining at the moment in the southwest. You only need to look outside. But the weather will change tonight. A wind from the south will bring warm, sunny weather tomorrow to the Scilly Isles, Cornwall and South Devon. In North Devon it will still be cloudy and you will have some rain in the morning and afternoon. But in the evening it will be warm and sunny there, too. I have a message for some kids on Exmoor. I hope they are listening to the radio this morning. They are pupils from Thomas Tallis School in Greenwich, London. They phoned the studio yesterday to tell us that they are fed up. They have been here for four days and it has rained every day! One of them asked: 'Does it rain here every day?' Well, the answer is 'No – sometimes it snows!' It's April and that means rain in this part of the country. But don't worry, kids. The day after tomorrow will be really nice. And it will stay like that for the next week. So have fun and enjoy your trip.

Unit 7   S. 77/ex. 8   Let's listen: Ready for Limerick

The Lehmann family are on a plane heading for Dublin airport

Christoph: Mum, if we have time, we'll go to Dublin again, right? Can we go soon?
Mrs Lehmann: Don't worry, Christoph. We'll go to Dublin. But first I want to quietly spend some time in Limerick.
Christoph: Spend some time in that dump!
Mr Lehmann: Hey! Don't forget all the great castles there. If the O'Brien's ghost isn't at the farmhouse, I'm sure we'll find a ghost in one of the castles.
Mrs Lehmann: And I'm sure you and Hannah will quickly find friends there. Mrs O'Brien says there are a lot of friendly children near them.
Hannah: Oh, Mum. Look down there. Isn't it beautiful? Everything is so green.
Mrs Lehmann: And look at all the lakes. Fantastic.
Mr Lehmann: I will happily go to every lake in Ireland with you.
Christoph: Lakes and lots of green. That sounds just great.
Girl: Excuse me. I heard that you are going to Limerick. I live there. There's a street fair on Friday. Here's some information about it.
Mrs Lehmann: Thank you. If we have time, maybe we'll go there. But maybe we'll go to Dublin on Friday.
Christoph: Oh no, we'll come. We've seen Dublin already. We can't wait to get to Limerick.
Hannah: That's funny! He has changed his plans very quickly. Suddenly he loves Limerick.

Orange Line 2

Inhaltsverzeichnis der CD zum Hörverstehen
Hörverstehenstexte aus Workbook und Schülerbuch

Track	Workbook Seite	Übung	Text/Übungstitel
1	4	3	Let's listen: Love or hate?
2	9	15	Let's listen: A lunch problem
3	15	3	Let's listen: Plans for the weekend
4	20	17	Let's listen: What Sam tells Lisa
5	28	3	Let's listen: 'Friends' last night
6	32	12	Let's listen: Parts of the body
7	32	13	Let's listen: Tom's day
8	38	3	Let's listen: What's for supper?
9	43	13	Let's listen: Five times a day
10	52	3	Let's listen: Terry's new webcam
11	58	14	Let's listen: Don't worry!
12	67	10	Let's listen: Three days later
13	75	3	Let's listen: What's wrong?
14	77	8	Let's listen: Ready for Limerick

Track	Schülerbuch Seite	Übung	Text/Übungstitel
15	17	2	Sounds: [dʒ] or [g]?
16	17	3	A poem: Down under in Australia
17–19	18–19	Story	You're boy mad, Emma!
20	29	4	Sounds: [t], [d] or [ɪd] at the end?
21–24	30–31	Story	That's why Barker barked!
25	32	1	Let's listen: Numbers and pounds
26	43	3	Sounds: Same sound, different spelling
27–30	44–45	Story	We're watching you!
31–33	56–57	Story	Sport can be dangerous!
34	58	1	Let's listen: A picture rhyme
35	69	2	Sounds: Which word was it?
36–38	70–71	Story	Where's my bag?
39	80	3	Let's listen: The signs of the zodiac
40	81	3	Let's listen: Mr Rose's tongue twister
41	81	4	Sounds: Which letter is missing?
42	82–83	Story	The Rescue
43	94–95	Story	Things that go bump in the night!
44–49	110–113	Text	Robin Hood and his merry band

Gesamtspielzeit: 77'29"